Self-Esteem In the Workplace

THE KEY TO POSITIVE EMPLOYEE RELATIONS

Joseph L. Richardson, B.S.
With
Joan L. Richardson, B.A., M.A.

Self-esteem in the Workplace
THE KEY TO POSITIVE EMPLOYEE RELATIONS

Copyright © 2010 by Joseph L. Richardson
All rights reserved

Printed in the United States of American

ISBN – 1453768742

No part of this book may not be reproduced in any form
unless written permission is granted from the author.
No electronic reproductions, information storage,
or retrieval systems may be used or applied to
any part of this book without written permission
from the author.

**To order a copy of this book please visit
Amazon.com
Books-A-Million.com
Barnes & Noble.com**

To contact the author for reproduction
requests, comments or corrections:
jrichard35@cfl.rr.com

Contents

Chapter:

1. IT HURTS TO SEE A CO-WORKER CRY.

2. WHAT IS SELF-ESTEEM, AND HOW DO WE GET IT?

3. I FEEL GOOD ABOUT MYSELF—EXCEPT...

4. SOME OF ME IS RED—SOME OF ME IS BLUE. (Self examination)

5. WHAT HAVE I LEARNED AND WHERE DO WE GO FROM HERE?

6. FINDING THE NEW EMPLOYEE

7. HERE I AM—WHAT NOW?

8. TELL ME WHAT TO DO AND HOW TO DO IT. (Training)

9. TALK WITH ME—NOT TO ME. (Communication)

10. HOW AM I DOING? (Performance Appraisal)

11. GIVE ME A TARGET. (Goal Setting)

12. YOU WANT ME TO DO THAT? (Delegation)

13. IF YOU ARE OUR LEADER, GET OUT IN FRONT. (Leadership)

14. WHAT IS THIS THING CALLED MOTIVATION?

15. THE PRESENT—IS GONE. (Time Management)

16. WHAT HAVE YOU DONE? WHAT ARE YOU GOING TO DO?

ACKNOWLEDGEMENTS

I could not have written this book without the support and assistance of my wife, Joan, a Psychotherapist with over 30 years in social work including more than twenty years in private practice. As a final project toward her Master's degree in counseling she developed a program designed to aid children develop a healthy, high self-esteem. After going into private practice she gave workshops on the subject of self-esteem and counseled many individuals who displayed symptoms of low self-esteem.

Her work kindled my own interest in the subject and prompted me to look at self-esteem as a factor in supervision, management, and leadership. Her expertise and guidance was vital to the development of this book—especially the first several chapters that take the reader through the definition of self-esteem and the introspection and acceptance of self. My grateful thanks to this intelligent, self-assured, and generous lady who has shared my life for the last fifty-five years.

I should also thank managers and supervisors I have known and observed over the years that provided many of the examples used in this book—good and bad.

J.L. Richardson, 2010

Preface

This book was written especially for the first-level supervisor, those who directly supervise the people—the grunts—that do the productive work of an organization, but may well be helpful for those at higher levels of the organization. The usual method of selecting employees to be promoted to the position of first-level supervisor is to determine who has the highest level of technical expertise in the organization with little or no regard to that person's ability to lead or to merely get along with co-workers. Too often they are given no—or very minimal—training in supervision. They are free to make all the mistakes they have learned from those who have supervised them in the past.

During my nearly thirty-six years with the federal government—over twenty-five in supervisory and management positions—I have had the opportunity to work for, work with, and observe a variety of approaches to supervision and management. I have seen a range from very good to horrible. I have drawn on these experiences and observations in writing this book. Some of the worst examples I cite are actual instances. In those cases I have changed the names of those involved to protect the innocent and to preserve my own skin in the unlikely event that one of them would read a book that might result in their changing the way they deal with their subordinates.

Because I have been unable to find any generic word that could be used in place of the awkward he/she, his/hers, him/her, etc. I have used both masculine and feminine pronouns with the intent that the reader would understand that they represent a person of either gender. One member of the writers' group of which I am a member said it seemed from my writing that, in general, the females were better supervisors than the males. I assure the reader that I did not intend to give that impression. I have observed and been subjected to female supervisors who bashed their workers with the worst of them. Recently, another member asked the difference between a supervisor and a manager. My reply:

The manager has four basic functions (some argue that there are five or even six, but I like to simplify). They are: planning, organizing, directing and evaluating. The supervisor also has four basic functions: directing, evaluating, organizing, and planning. Are the two similar? No. It is a matter of emphasis. The work is normally apportioned in the order shown above. The manager spends most of his time planning, while the supervisor spends most of her time directing. Next comes organizing for the manager, and evaluating for the supervisor. The manager spends less of his time directing and evaluating, and the supervisor spends less of her time planning and organizing. This is logical because the higher in an organization a person climbs, the fewer the people who report directly to her. She becomes progressively farther removed from the people who turn out the work for the organization.

I will be happy if this book helps just one person become a better supervisor or manager.

2

Chapter 1

IT HURTS TO SEE A CO-WORKER CRY

It hurts to see a co-worker cry. I saw it happen. I saw an intelligent, capable, and experienced professional driven to tears by the callous, overbearing, unfeeling actions of his supervisor. He had just suffered a vicious verbal attack in front of his peers and officials from other offices in the organization. His tears were tears of frustration, humiliation, embarrassment, and worst of all, a severely injured self-esteem.

What error of omission or commission had he made that called for such an attack by the supervisor? **NONE.** He had done exactly what he had been told to do, but because of poor communication or a misunderstanding, his actions had not been what the supervisor wanted. "Rob" (not his real name) and the rest of us in the office had been given our instructions by two intermediaries who had no assigned supervisory relationship over the members of our group. The supervisor consistently used them to convey messages to the employees instead of talking to them himself.

Rather than ask Rob why he was doing what he was doing or ask the intermediaries if Rob was doing what they had told him to do, the supervisor chose to attack him on a very personal basis. Next, he turned his tirade on the rest of us, shouting that he never got what he wanted and that we'd all better learn by the next review. He then left the room and slammed the door.

The rest of us gathered our materials and went back to our cubicles. I looked for Rob. I found him standing, quietly looking out the window. There were tears running down his cheeks.

Deep inside I hurt because I, along with the others, had been unfairly attacked. I hurt, too for Rob who had been so brutally attacked in front of the others.

None of us had been totally surprised by the supervisor's actions. Everyone in the office had experienced or witnessed his tyrannical outbursts, but this time the attack was more severe than any we had seen in the past. As a rule, he showed little regard for the people working under his supervision. He was totally autocratic and he could never accept the fact that he might be wrong on an issue or that he could make an error. In three years I never heard him praise an employee for a job well done. His line was: "I don't pat people on the back for doing what they are supposed to do. They aren't supposed to make mistakes."

Who suffered from the incident? Rob, of course, suffered a great deal, but every employee suffered humiliation and some loss of self-esteem because his/her capability to do the job had been attacked.

The two who had given the instructions that Rob had followed lost the respect of the workers by not interrupting and admitting that Rob had followed their instructions. They also lost self-esteem because the employees viewed them as unreliable and non-supportive.

The supervisor lost the respect, the support, and the loyalty of everyone who was present—not just his own employees. And what of the self-esteem of the supervisor? A supervisor with a healthy self-esteem does not feel the need to be autocratic nor resort to temper "explosions." He does not feel threatened by others so he does not have a need to feel superior to his employees nor to win through intimidation.

The supervisor with high self-esteem would have been able to stop Rob's presentation in a non-threatening manner and ask why he was deviating from the established procedure and he would have listened to Rob's answer. If the intermediaries had misunderstood his instructions, he could have talked to them later about the problem. He also would have been able to listen to Rob's presentation with an open mind to determine whether or not the "new" way would have been just as effective as the old with the benefit of saving both preparation and presentation time.

The organization lost a great deal. It lost the loyalty and good work of well-qualified and effective personnel. Within a few months it lost all the employees who had been present at the meeting.

The devastating result of the incident was the loss to the self-esteem of all employees who were present, even the two who had given the instructions. Only a person with very strong self-esteem could have been attacked the way Rob had been without some negative effect. A person with low or a fragile self-esteem could suffer lasting scars from that type treatment.

My reason for writing about the incident is to give the reader an extreme example of how the behavior of a supervisor can destroy the self-esteem of an individual or the collective self-esteem of a group. Usually, the things a supervisor does that adversely affect the self-esteem of an employee are much less obvious, and the supervisor is not aware that he has treated a person in a way that might have a negative effect. Many are oblivious to the self-esteem needs of their workers and to the fact that they might do something that has a negative effect. They continue their behavior and they and management wonder why production isn't as high as it could be and why the employee turnover rate is higher than it should be.

By understanding self-esteem, learning esteem-building behavior and practicing that behavior, a supervisor can help build in his employees a feeling of self worth that will encourage them to give their best to the organization and to have a feeling of performance capability that will permit them to strive for more demanding work with a higher level of responsibility.

Not every employee will be helped to that degree, but those who are recipients of the supervisor's esteem-enhancing behavior will appreciate the SUPER in supervision.

Think back to all the people with whom you have worked over the years—even schoolmates. Remember those who made the greatest impression on you because of their positive attitude toward the organization, management, their co-workers and the work being done. Think particularly of those who always seemed to be able to handle any assignment with little or no hesitation and did the work with a minimum of supervision or direction—those who always seemed to be able to accomplish the most with the least help. Think about their personalities. They were the people who displayed a great deal of self-confidence. They were the people who had high self-esteem. They knew their capabilities without over-rating themselves or moping about what they could have done if they "...had just been given a chance." They may have been extroverts or introverts, gregarious or quiet loners, brilliant or of average intelligence, but they did have one attribute in common: they knew and valued themselves and their capabilities, and they had accepted their shortcomings (as they saw them) without self-flagellation. They had high self-esteem.

Next, think about those individuals who were never self-starters, those who had to be constantly pushed to reach minimally acceptable performance. They may have been the people who had mastered a fairly simple job that they performed at an acceptable level, but were content to remain on that job rather than risk taking one with greater challenge or higher level of responsibility. They probably were the ones who rarely, if ever volunteered for extra work–even with overtime pay. They would never have had the courage to ask their boss for a raise or for a job with more potential. They were the ones who other employees never felt were carrying their part of the workload.

Think of those people neither as poor workers who never carried their part of the work nor as people who were not very bright. Many of them may have been very intelligent, but were suffering from low self-esteem, self-esteem so low that they actually felt inferior to others in the group. They may have thought themselves incapable of doing more demanding work and were, unfortunately, incapable of expressing their own needs and desires. Think of them as people who "hid their light under a basket" and were never able to display their true potential to their supervisor, to their co-workers, or—worst of all—to themselves.

Think back to the attitudes of the other workers—even yourself—toward employees with such low self-esteem. Were you and the others supportive, encouraging, and helpful, or did you "put down" or even ignore them?

This writer has four goals in researching, developing, and writing this book:

First, to give the supervisor information on self-esteem—what it is, what affects the level of our self-esteem, and the conditions required for a person to develop high self-esteem.

Second, to bring to the supervisor tools that can be used to evaluate his or her own self-esteem, recognize strengths and weaknesses, determine areas in which he/she needs self acceptance, identify areas that need strengthening, and to provide methods that can be used to strengthen those areas.

Third, to help the supervisor understand how his actions and attitudes can affect his employees' level of self-esteem. To help him examine his own actions and attitudes to determine whether he is helping his employees become the best they can be by boosting their self-esteem or if he is holding them back from becoming better employees and living full lives as a result of his esteem-damaging behavior.

Fourth, to give the supervisor, through examples, methods of interacting with her employees in ways that will enhance their self-esteem and help them achieve higher levels of productivity, competence, and confidence.

The next chapter is devoted to learning what is meant by self-esteem, what makes up our self-esteem, and the conditions that must be present for a person to have high self-esteem.

Chapter 2

WHAT IS SELF-ESTEEM – AND HOW DO WE GET IT?

The American Heritage Dictionary of the English Language defines self-esteem as "Pride in oneself." While some may consider this an adequate definition, self-esteem is actually a very complex and important part of our makeup. Our self-esteem measures how we view ourselves in relation to the world in which we live and to the others who live in our world. Our self-esteem is the grade we give ourselves as individuals.

Most of us fill our mental report cards with some A's, some B's some C's and in a few particular areas, lower grades. The person with low self-esteem, on the other hand, starts at the bottom with the red F's, may give himself a few C's, fewer B's, and even fewer—if any—A's.

Self-esteem gives us our opinions as to whether or not we are capable of accomplishing much or little in our world. It gives us an unsolicited, and often erroneous, evaluation of our intelligence, our talents, our abilities, and our potential.

Self-esteem is a paradox. It is the strength within us that tells us we can take on challenges and risks with a firm belief in our ability to win. It gives us confidence that we can challenge and overcome superior forces, but it also is the cause of butterflies in our stomachs, the tremble in our knees, and the tightness in our throats when we are asked to speak to the local Cub Scout pack. It can be as tough as a diamond or as fragile as crystal. The conditions necessary for a person to have healthy, high self-esteem have been described in many ways. Dr. Harris Clemes, Ph.D. and Dr. Reynold Bean, Ed.M. in their books on developing self-esteem describe only four conditions. The degree to which these conditions are met reflects the level of a person's self-esteem. For a person to have high self-esteem, all of the following conditions must be met.

CONNECTIVENESS
POWER (CONTROL)
UNIQUENESS
MODELS

CONNECTIVENES OR SENSE OF BELONGING:

A person needs a feeling of belonging to a family, to a group, or to some unit—even if is called a gang—to connect with the people who are important in her life. In the workplace this means having a feeling of belonging to or being a part of the group of co-workers with whom she works. Employees who are treated by their supervisor as expendable, work-producing units rather than human beings who are making valuable contributions to the organization will have little feeling of being a part of the work group. They will have little feeling of value to the organization, will have a low level of self-esteem as measured by their work contribution and, as a result, will have little or no feeling of dedication to the organization. The employee who has no feeling of belonging to the organization may well become the withdrawn, low production loner in the group.

The role of the supervisor in giving the employee a sense of belonging to the group should be obvious. The supervisor should, from the time the employee comes into the group, let the employee know that the work he is doing is important in meeting the goals of the organization and how his work fits into the overall operation. The employee who enters a job and is simply told, "sit here and do this," and is ignored by the other workers and the supervisor—except to be handed additional work—will find little satisfaction in her work and will have a low sense of self-worth because of her apparent lack of acceptance in and importance to the work group.

A SENSE OF POWER OR CONTROL

A sense of power or control comes from a person's feeling that he possesses the skills, the resources, the capability, and the opportunity to influence his own life circumstances, make choices, and be responsible for his actions. When an employee believes he is being denied the right to make decisions affecting his work even though he feels he has the ability to correctly make those decisions, and that his destiny is totally under the control of others, the employee may resort to other methods of gaining control such as becoming rebellious or argumentative.

When a person has a sense of some control over his work and his life situation, he will be willing to put forth greater effort, won't be as easily stopped when confronted with problems, and will be willing to work longer and harder to meet a goal. In addition, people with a sense of control over their lives have fewer illnesses and recover more quickly from those they do have. They react to fewer events in a stress-producing manner, so have fewer stress-related illnesses.

When the worker is given a feeling of some degree of control over his job and his destiny, such as making decisions on some matters concerning his work or being delegated authority to carry out certain responsibilities or approve certain actions without consulting his supervisor, he will have a greater sense of control over the work and his future. When he has some vision of potential career growth within the organization based on his performance, he develops a sense of having some responsibility for and control over the future of his career. The supervisor, thus, the organization that gives to their employees these feelings of control or power, will have a better satisfied, better working, and more dedicated work group.

A SENSE OF UNIQUENESS:

Every human being wants and needs to be treated as a unique individual: one who possesses his own set of physical characteristics, talents, skills, knowledge, thoughts and opinions. He needs to recognize his own uniqueness, but, even more, he needs the recognition of his parents, his peers, his co-workers, his supervisor, and even strangers that he is an individual unlike any other person on earth.

If a supervisor fails to recognize the uniqueness of employees under his direction, he will deny each of them the opportunity to develop this sense or condition necessary for them to have high self-esteem. He will also deny the organization the benefit of the unique capabilities that each employee could contribute to the organization.

The supervisor, who boasts, "I treat all my employees alike," is either fooling himself or is a very difficult person to work for.

A supervisor works with a group of individuals who are administratively assigned to her organizational entity, but that supervisor does not supervise or motivate <u>the group.</u> Instead, he supervises and attempts to motivate <u>the individuals who make up that group.</u> To do so he must recognize the differences in these people in order to identify their individual needs and to identify their best, most productive qualities in order to use them to the fullest for the good of both the organization and the person.

Military basic training attempts to cast all members of a group into a single fighting unit. Everyone is treated the same. They all receive the same training, fire the same rifles, perform the same dirty work, and pass the same inspections. Ultimately, it is the rigidity of the training that brings out the uniqueness of the individual soldier. Because of the individual's need for recognition as a unique person, those with the strongest need to display this uniqueness, will emerge as the strongest, the best shot, or the informal leader of the organization. Those are the soldiers with the high self-esteem necessary to show themselves as having unique skills, talents, strengths.

Each shows his uniqueness, even that of being the best scrounger in the outfit. The wise commander recognizes these traits as they emerge and takes advantage of this knowledge in order to build the best possible unit.

This is true for the supervisor of any organization. To develop the best unit or group possible, he must utilize the knowledge, skills, and talent available to him. It is incumbent on the supervisor to help each employee to display his uniqueness, to recognize those traits, and to use them the same as he would utilize other resources available to him. Every supervisor should realize that only by bringing out the best in his people will he ever be able to demonstrate the best in himself by utilizing <u>all</u> resources available to him.

A SENSE OF MODELS:

To acquire good self-regard or self-esteem a person must be able to distinguish between right and wrong and between appropriate and inappropriate behavior.

As children we have role models who influence us in forming our behavior standards. We look to the ways our parents, other adults, and our peers act or react in situations and derive our standards from what we see and hear. The key to developing a good set of standards is to have role models who act and react consistently in a manner that is acceptable to society. Later, as we mature and have various experiences, we build on the standards we have developed as children by observing the responses of others to our actions. The role model who is inconsistent in the manner in which he acts or reacts sends confusing messages that fail to provide a solid base upon which we can develop our own standards of conduct.

In the work situation, an employee must be able to look first and foremost to her supervisor as a role model who provides appropriate and correct behavior on the job. The supervisor who demands punctuality but frequently arrives late for work, one who misses deadlines, or one who demands that employees keep their noses to the grindstone for eight full hours a day –or even more—while he chats, reads, disappears for long periods of time, or otherwise wastes company time cannot serve as an acceptable role model for his employees. The supervisor who works by the old adage, " Don't do as I do, do as I say ," may find that his subordinates do as he <u>says do</u> while he is present, but quickly resort to <u>doing as he does</u> when he leaves the work area for even a short time. They may feel, albeit unconsciously, that goofing off, leaving the work area, or chatting is actually acceptable behavior because that is the behavior that has been modeled by their supervisor.

The supervisor who displays enthusiasm, and interest in the work, a sense of value to the organization and its goals, and observes the rules of the business, will serve as a positive role model who can expect the same behavior from his employees as he gives the organization. Model the behavior you desire.

Under certain circumstances, each of us has had or will have feelings of inadequacy or self-doubt. These feelings likely reflect situations that took place earlier in our life when we didn't perform up to our expectations or to the expectations of others who were important in our lives. In most instances we brace ourselves and go ahead and try, not because we have overcome these feelings, but in spite of the fact that we have them. If we do well we will most likely be elated and that particular situation will no longer present so great a challenge. If we do not perform as well as we think we should have, most of us have the ability and the strength to set aside the disappointment in ourselves and accept the fact that we may not be as skilled, talented, and trained in that particular area as some others might be. We can do that without harboring a continuing feeling of inadequacy and without labeling ourselves as failures. But what about the person with low self-esteem?

A person suffering from low self-esteem may feel inadequate or incapable of meeting the demands placed upon her, particularly the demands of a job that presents any degree of challenge. That person may reach for nothing but the least demanding, lowest paying job or she may resort to the life of the chronically unemployed or under employed. He may see no future for himself in a society that honors, rewards, and virtually idolizes the high achiever.

The person with low self-esteem may view any situation that presents even the slightest challenge as having the potential of showing the world his inadequacy and inability, and the potential to add one more failure to a life filled with failure. Low self-esteem results in fear. It is fear of life's demands that robs him of the power to say, "yes" to life's challenges.

Unfortunately, when a person grows up with these degrading opinions of himself, it is extremely difficult to overcome these poor self-evaluations. Often, it cannot be done without the help of others who know and care about that person.

In the business world there will always be employees who never live up to their true potential because they never have a true picture of what they can accomplish. They never believe themselves capable of meeting the challenges imposed by more complex work or higher levels of responsibility. Employees who live in this self-imposed world of restricted performance delude themselves, delude their families, delude the organization in which they work, and delude society by not giving them the products of their minds and talents that would be possible if they could shed their fear of failure and live up to their true potential.

HOW OUR SELF-ESTEEM IS DEVELOPED

Why do so many people grow up with such poor regard for themselves in a world filled with opportunities? Our feelings of self-regard/self-esteem are rooted in the nurturing, the attitudes, the responses, and the acceptance of us by our parents, our teachers, other adults, and our peers during our early years.

PARENTAL INPUT

We are all familiar with stories of parents who physically abuse their children with beating, burning, scalding, etc. but we hear little of those who emotionally abuse their children with actions and words. These are the parents who ignore the children or treat them with indifference, or destroy their possibility of developing positive self-esteem by convincing the child that, "...you'll never amount to anything," "...you can never do anything right," "...you're too stupid to ever learn to do that." Fortunately, these parents are relatively few, but such abuse frequently results in a debilitating low self-esteem in a person who could have accomplished a great deal if he had not been constantly told that he couldn't.

Most parents would never consciously do anything to hurt their children. They might, however, injure them unconsciously by comparing their child's accomplishments, talents, or appearance with siblings or peers who make higher grades, throw a baseball better, or are chosen Miss Something-or-other. Even a casual remark such as, "I wish you were as popular as Mary," can be a devastating put down for a child who interprets the remark as, "You are not pretty or as popular as Mary," or "I wish Mary were my daughter."

Making positive remarks and responses, giving praise, actively listening, being a good role model, and using positive, consistent discipline are important factors in helping a child develop high self-esteem.

TEACHER INPUT

Teachers play an important role in the formation of child's self-esteem. They can help build a child's positive self-esteem by encouraging and helping, or they can make an unsure student even unsure of herself. They sometimes make remarks about a student's work or compare the student with one who makes higher grades. The target child may take the remark to mean that she is stupid, or a failure, or that she is incapable of doing the work.

An "F" on a test means only that the student did not meet the teacher's standard for a passing grade on those particular questions on that particular subject on that particular day. But the student who frequently receives F's may brand herself a failure not just on those test scores, but in all phases of her life. She may picture herself as a failure to the extent that she develops a failure complex and will not be willing to risk doing anything because she believes she is destined to fail. Actually, she may be perfectly capable of performing very well if she would put as much energy into risking as in convincing herself that she will fail if she tries.

PEER/SIBLING INPUT

Our reaction to the treatment we receive from our peers as we grow up has a direct relationship to the level of our self-esteem. Children are very frank in what they say and can be brutal in their treatment of their peers. If a child hears from his siblings or schoolmates that he is stupid, or a nerd, or that he is funny looking, it can be difficult for that child to ignore the epithets, so they may become a part of his personal belief system. Being the last chosen for a game becomes a loud and clear statement that he is not as good as the others in the game. In that case, the child does not have a sense of belonging to the group, of having any power or control, or models, and is not in a position at that time to demonstrate his uniqueness. His feelings may extend to other parts of his life.

YOUR ROLE AS A SUPERVISOR.

An insensitive supervisor can easily add to a person's self-imposed concept of his inadequacy. If an employee is poorly or improperly trained he may be prone to errors from the beginning of his employment. When those errors are immediately and perhaps rudely, pointed out, the employee with low self-esteem may find his negative feeling about himself further verified. The result can be that he will become extremely cautious in his work. This may result in a supervisor's evaluation that he is not only prone to errors but is too slow in his work. The stress from his anxiety in the work place can result in even more errors and more cautious performance.

As his belief of inadequacy is further verified by the words and actions of the supervisor, the next result may be habitual absence or tardiness as a way of avoiding more negatives. He may become the "job hopper" who moves from one job to another until he finds one that makes few demands and offers little potential.

In some cases, a person with low self-esteem may find an area in which he can perform well. He may then over-compensate by becoming an over-achiever in that particular part of his life in order to make up for the self-ordained deficiencies in other aspects of his life.

Most of us do not suffer from such low self-esteem as those described above, but some who appear to have healthy self-esteem may have a problem but hide it well. They may find it difficult to meet people, to take on new tasks, to go through a job interview, or to do other things necessary to get ahead and fully participate in the activities of their world. They have to push themselves through a lifetime of anxiety to reach only a fraction of their potential.

The supervisor's role in developing self-esteem in their employees is one of many characters. She must become the supervisor who maintains responsibility for the work of the group while serving as the role model, mentor, trainer, coach, and cheerleader, for the group and the individuals who make up that group. She recognizes good work, accomplishment, and potential with even more enthusiasm than she recognizes errors or lapses in judgment. She praises in public, disciplines in private.

THE SUPERVISOR'S SELF-ESTEEM

Feelings of inadequacy are not limited to the lower level personnel in an organization. Most often, the tyrannical, autocratic, abrasive, perfectionist supervisor or manager is attempting to hide a deep-rooted poor self-concept that makes him doubt his deserving of his position. By being autocratic and demanding, he shields himself from questions, challenges, or input from his employees whom he fears will uncover his inability or lack of knowledge. Because of his intimidating behavior, workers may carry out orders or instructions that they know are wrong, or do their work in a prescribed way even though there are better, more efficient ways to do it in order to avoid further intimidation or even retaliation. They certainly would not feel free to bring the supervisor's errors to his attention.

In this situation, employees have been known to resort to what is called "malicious compliance." The supervisor gives an order that will, if carried out as he directs, cause repercussions and possibly get the supervisor in trouble with his own boss. The knowing employees smile at each other and carefully, openly, carry out their supervisor's instructions to the letter.

The other extreme of supervisory behavior influenced by low self-esteem is the boss who is never able to make a decision. Frequently she becomes the private office recluse who has little personal contact with his employees, sometimes abdicating her supervisory authority and responsibility to a stronger subordinate who becomes the informal but actual leader of the group.

The perfectionist may be covering up his feelings of inferiority by attempting to appear perfect in his work and demanding perfection from his employees. His own perfectionism may come in the form of something relatively minor in the work of the group, such as punctuation in correspondence. But he may attempt to demand perfection from the workers in all parts of their jobs. What he doesn't realize is that having to be right all the time has an opposite effect of making the workers fear being wrong all the time, thus negating their willingness to risk or to find new and better ways to do the work. The more a supervisor demands perfection, the more imperfection he will find.

SUMMARY:

We have explored the four conditions that are required for high self-esteem and the various elements—parental input, teacher input, peer input, and supervisor's input—that are factors in shaping our self-esteem. We have found that, as supervisors, our own self-esteem affects the way we interact with our employees. If our actions and attitudes are esteem damaging rather than esteem enhancing, the negative results can not only cause damage to self-esteem of the individual employee, but also can negatively affect the efficiency and effectiveness of the organization. The supervisor with high self-esteem never looks upon his employees as threats to himself or to his position.

THE NEXT STEP IS TO EXAMINE OUR OWN SELF-ESTEEM
1. Recognize our strengths.
2. Recognize those areas of our self-esteem that call merely for acceptance on our part.
3. Find those areas that need to be and can be improved.
4. Explore ways to improve our attitudes toward ourselves.

Chapter 3

I FEEL GOOD ABOUT MYSELF...EXCEPT...

For you to understand how an employee's self-esteem can affect her attitude and her performance on the job, you should first examine your own self-esteem. Only by recognizing your own attitudes toward yourself and facing your own inadequacies can you understand how some of your employees can have the same kinds of feelings about some areas of their own lives. Then you will be able to help them overcome some of the negative beliefs they have about themselves. It is difficult for a person to improve his self-esteem without the help of someone who cares about him. You can be that caring person.

Self-esteem problems fall into two general categories: situational problems and characterological problems.

SITUATIONAL PROBLEMS

Situational problems are those that manifest themselves in certain situations such as meeting new people, speaking before a group, playing in certain sports, facing change, taking tests, etc. They are problems because the person has never developed confidence in her ability to deal with those situations. She becomes afraid that she will fail and be unable to perform as well as she thinks she should—or in the worst case—may be frightened into inaction because of her fear of failure.

The situations that present a problem to you may pose no threat to your closest friend. By the same token, her problems may lie in situations that you enjoy. Each of us has his or her own personal set of situational problems that were developed through our negative experiences. Fortunately, situational problems, while the most common type, are the most easily improved by the person who wishes to change, and the type that can be helped by the positive attitude and action of a caring person such as a super supervisor.

CHARACTEROLOGICAL PROBLEMS

The second type of self-esteem problem is the characterological problem. This means that the person has low self-esteem because he perceives himself as having serious flaws in his character. He may see himself as a bad person because of some early negative circumstance that affected his very being. While some people may develop this type problem as the result of their perception of constant failure, they are usually developed as the result of the negative influence of others in their lives. Those with characterological problems are the victims of emotional abuse coming from such "put downs" as, "You're no good," 'You'll never amount to anything," "You aren't worth anything."

It is unlikely that a person with severe characterological based problems would be able to reach a supervisory or managerial position or any position of leadership or responsibility. These attitudes are deep-rooted and difficult to overcome. A person with this type problem should be encouraged to seek professional help.

In less severe cases, the person may be helped by the encouragement of a supervisor who is concerned about him, wants him to see the fallacy in his thinking, desires to see him change his attitude toward himself, and wants him to realize his own potential.

Characterological problems often become self-fulfilling prophecies. The person who perceives himself as non-deserving or as a bad person will often live the life style that verifies these perceptions. If he does not consider himself deserving of the good things in life, he will neither strive for those things nor be willing to take the risks that could result in his legitimately acquiring those things. Criminal behavior could result. He has been negatively programmed for life unless strong measures are taken to help him, that person can be helped by others but only if he wants to change himself.

HOW HIGH IS <u>YOUR</u> SELF-ESTEEM?

The following exercise will help you take a good look at your own self-esteem. In this exercise it is vital that you be perfectly honest and open. If you feel good about yourself in certain situations or you are good at doing something, admit it. This is neither bragging nor a display of ego; it is a part of examining your attitude toward yourself. If you concentrate only on the negatives or the areas in which you are uncomfortable, you will commit the same error as many people with low self-esteem. You will not consider your accomplishments and abilities to be worthwhile and meaningful, and you will emphasize the negatives and under emphasize the positives in your life.

If you do not feel comfortable or confident in a situation, face up to that fact. Respond as you actually feel. You cannot improve yourself in areas that you refuse to recognize to be in need of change. You cannot really love yourself if you reject a part of yourself instead of understanding and accepting that part—even though it may be a trait you dislike.

The responses to this exercise are yours alone. Sharing them might influence the way you respond for fear of revealing something about yourself that you would rather keep secret. Being honest in your responses is the only way that you will be able to identify both good and poor attitudes toward yourself. Only then can you accept those things you cannot change and work toward improving areas that are affecting your life to the point that you recognize the need to change.

Begin with the understanding that this exercise is not one to be completed in a few minutes or even a few hours. It may, in fact, take several days. You will not be able—in a short time—to think of all your traits, abilities, skills, talents, that you consider positive or to identify all those traits that you consider negative. Take time to develop an introspective attitude. When you face various situations from day to day you should find yourself thinking of those situations in terms of your confidence or comfort level and how you perform.

FIRST, get yourself a large piece of white paper—the bigger, the better. A full sheet of poster board is ideal. This is an important exercise and a small piece of paper may tend to limit your responses as you see the paper being covered with your notations.

SECOND, get three felt tip markers, one black, one red, and one blue. Print your full name in the middle of the sheet in black and draw a circle around it. Print your name large enough that you can read it from some distance. This exercise is about you and only you so begin by showing that you are the important person who is the subject of this exercise.

THIRD, sit back and start to think of yourself in terms of talent, skills, abilities, things you can do, personal traits that are valuable to you. These are not to be solely related to your work even though this book addresses itself to the work situation. In this exercise you are looking at the total you. It takes in all facets of your work, and all facets of your life affect your work.

Start by thinking of your strengths: those things you are good at that make you feel good about yourself. Think in terms of: I am, I can, I'm good at, I'm comfortable with, etc. As you discover your strengths write them on the sheet using your **red** marker. You use red for these strengths because red is a warm color and the responses you write down in red are those that make you feel warm or good about yourself.

You may start with something as simple as, "I am good at English grammar." Next you may find something such as, "I am punctual," or "I am good at repairing things," "I have a good sense of humor," "My work reports are well written and complete," "I work well with others," "I work well with children," "I'm a good cook."

When you write down your positive traits, scatter them around the sheet of paper. Don't reserve the top of the paper for those things you consider your strong points. Life isn't compartmentalized; any part of your life has an effect on all the other parts of your life, so your responses should not be set up in plots of good and bad.

As you write down your positive traits, they will begin to remind you of situations in which you feel uncomfortable or inadequate—areas in which you feel that you need improvement. As you recognize these improvable traits write them down on your paper using the **blue** marker. (Let's not call them negative or bad because they are not negative, they are merely parts of your being, and they can be changed or improved.) Write these down using your blue marker because they are the responses that tend to make us less than fully happy with ourselves. Again, scatter them about the paper. Mingle them in with the red entries. These traits are mingled in your life with those you feel good about, so mingle them on your paper.

Take your time making entries on your paper. You will probably start off with a rush and then slow down. As you think of more entries they will, in turn, trigger thoughts about others—both good and improvable. If your work on this sheet takes several days or even several weeks, that is okay. It means that you are putting a great deal of thought into your entries. The better, more thorough job you do in writing them down, the more you will begin to know about yourself and the better job you will be able to do in examining your self-esteem and identifying your "improvables."

TO VALUE YOURSELF, YOU MUST KNOW YOURSELF

If you are typical—and you most likely are—you will find that as you make your entries the sheet of paper will take on a predominately RED tone with fewer BLUE entries. If you find that the blue entries are predominate, you should stop, take a break, and think only of the things you can do and do them well. You may have not been honest with yourself, or you may have hesitated to say anything good about yourself. This is not the time to be timid.

Think of characteristics such as being friendly, trustworthy, helpful, etc. It is easy to forget these personal qualities in favor of talents and skills, but these qualities are part of your total makeup. Don't be shy about self-praise. Modesty about your good qualities, your accomplishments, and your abilities may reflect a lower than deserved self-esteem. Think about compliments you have received on your work, volunteer duties, dress, smile, voice, and appearance. You may consider some of these things too insignificant to write down. They're not. Get them down in that warm red.

Don't rush. Leave your sheet alone for a while, then come back and review what you have written down. When you are satisfied that you have made all the entries you can—red and blue—then, and only then, are you ready to go on to the next chapter and begin to analyze what you have written. You have probably already begun to learn some things about yourself, but you will learn others.

Chapter 4

SOME OF ME IS RED—
SOME OF ME IS BLUE

Now that you have studied your feelings about yourself and written those feelings on your big sheet of paper, it's time to look over what you have written and learn more about yourself.

If you are typical—and you probably are—your sheet has a good mix of red and blue entries with red being the predominate color. This indicates that you have generally healthy self-esteem. You have more points with which you are comfortable than you have things with which you are uncomfortable.

Now, get out three sheets of paper. Lined notebook paper is ideal. Title the three sheets as follows:

1. RED – MY STRENGTHS
2. BLUE – THINGS I AM NOT HAPPY ABOUT
3. BLUE – THINGS I CAN DO NOTHING ABOUT

On sheet number 2 write down all the BLUE entries from the large sheet. Again, check them off or line through them as you write them down.

Now, take time to compare the two sheets. You will probably find more entries on the "red" sheet than on the "blue" sheet. You will find that the things that are most important to you are on the "red" sheet. The things on the "blue" sheet are those that are less important. This is because we tend to create our lives around the things with which we are most comfortable and which we do well.

Now, take a closer look at the things you wrote on the "red" sheet. You may be surprised to find out how many things you can do well and how many good personal traits you have. You probably have more skills and talents than you ever suspected. These are the things that shape your life and your work.

If you detect a feeling of self-pride as you review this sheet it is perfectly all right. You should be proud of your good points. A healthy feeling of pride in oneself is a natural result of high self-esteem.

As you review the sheet put a "pride" star beside the items that are most important to you. If your paper begins to look like a flag with all those stars, that's okay, too. Those are the things that you do well and the things that build high self-esteem.

You might want to make a separate list of entries that are related. This may give you a valuable clue as to the type occupation that would be best for you. You may be better suited for a type of job different from the one you are in without ever realizing it. For instance, if you are good at math, have patience, work well alone, are good at logical thinking, you may be well suited for a job as a computer programmer-- with the proper training, of course.

Take your time. Learn some things about yourself.

After you have finished your sheet with the red entries, made your "pride" stars, and looked for related entries, it is time to take a look at the paper on which you made your blue entries.

Look first for any entries that are characterological. In the last chapter we learned that these are based on feelings of being unworthy or bad. An entry of that type would be one saying something like, "I don't deserve what I have in life," or, "I am not a good person." You probably will not find any of that type, but if you do, I recommend that you seek help from a mental health counselor. That type problem is deep-rooted and can have such a devastating effect on a person that I could not—would not-- presume to help you change those negative self-concepts through the simple methods that could be covered in a book such as this.

The next three steps you should take in reviewing the "blue" sheet are important. Follow the instructions completely.

1. Take out sheets No. 2., THINGS I AM NOT HAPPY ABOUT and No. 3, BLUE...THINGS I CAN DO NOTHING ABOUT. (Sheet No. 2 should be blank at this point).
2. Carefully examine each entry on the No. 2 sheet. Look for any entries that you cannot change, entries such as: "I am too short," "I am too tall," I am the wrong race," "I have freckles," "I am too old," etc. As you find these, write them on sheet No. 3 THINGS I CAN DO NOTHING ABOUT. As you write them on that sheet, line through them on sheet No. 2 with a felt tip marker or a dark pencil so that you can be sure you have written them all on sheet No. 3, and to be sure that you can no longer read them on sheet No. 2.
3. Read the entries you have written on sheet No. 3, THINGS I CAN DO NOTHING ABOUT.
4. Read each entry slowly and carefully. Recognize that these are the things you CANNOT change, things you can do nothing about. You cannot go back to your birth and be born to another family. You cannot go back and change the genes you inherited. You cannot change your race, your sex, your height, the date of your birth. You are stuck with those things, <u>so forget them.</u>
5. Hold sheet No. 3 in front of you, a hand at each upper corner. Grip those corners tightly. Move one hand toward you, the other away from you. RIP THE SHEET IN TWO. Put the two pieces in one stack and rip them again. Do this over and over until there is nothing but confetti. Hold the pieces in your cupped hands. Kiss all those useless bits of paper goodbye. Put them in a fireproof container and set them on fire.

6. Stir the bits of paper until there is nothing left but ash. Take the container out of doors and let the ashes blow to the wind.
7. Many successful people have been short, or old, or of the "wrong" sex or race or had other characteristics that could have held them back if they had wasted their time worrying about them or had convinced themselves that they were real handicaps. These types of things are merely excuses for not trying. They are not reasons for not doing what you want to do or being who you want to be. They are the things you must accept about yourself.

One of the most important factors in attaining a high degree of self-esteem is change. If you cannot accept them you may go through life using them as weapons against yourself.

You may be saying to yourself, "That's easy to say, but you probably don't have anything you don't like about yourself that you need to accept."

Well, I'm only 5'6'—short for a man—and I have a silver dollar size wine-colored birthmark on my neck just below my left jaw. Throughout high school I never dared ask a girl who was taller than I for a date (and many of them were taller), and I was very self-conscious about my birthmark. When I grew more mature I found that a plastic surgeon could remove the birthmark using what he called, "...a simple procedure." I procrastinated and as time went by I realized that removing it would not change the way I felt about myself. Now, sometimes when I am shaving, I rediscover the wine-colored mark as though I had never seen it before. It hasn't changed, but my attitude toward it has changed. (Note: Soon after finishing this book I did have it removed, but only after my dermatologist advised me that it had changed and appeared to be pre-cancerous.)

After high school I learned that some of the girls I wouldn't ask for a date would have gone out with me if only I had had the courage to ask them. Many of the people I have supervised over the years are taller than I—both men and women—and I have never felt insecure about supervising people who towered over me.

Both my sons are taller than I, and my wife isn't much shorter than I am. Using today's politically correct jargon, I may be considered "vertically challenged." Physical height isn't important, what is important is how you feel about yourself and how you use your talents, skills, knowledge and potential.

You've looked at the things that make your chest swell with pride—the things on your No.1 RED sheet, and you have looked at the things you can do nothing about on your No. 3 BLUE sheet—and torn that sheet apart and thrown the scraps away. Now it's time to go back and look at the remaining entries on your No. 2 BLUE SHEET.

Again, it's time for acceptance. When you review your blue sheet you must accept things you don't like about yourself or situations in which you are not comfortable. There are things that you think you do not do well. You must accept those facts because you can do nothing to change those things or correct them until you accept the fact that you have them and you can do something about them. You have taken the initial steps toward accepting and changing them by having the courage to be self-critical and introspective, picking up your blue marker, and writing them down.

Next, number in order of importance to you those things you truly want to change about yourself—things you will be willing to expend effort and resources to change. These are the items you want to change into assets or, at least, improve. For example: improve my writing skills, lose weight, improve job skills, handle myself better during job interviews, give better presentations, improve relationships with co-workers, spend more time with my family.

Understand that you must be willing to sacrifice whatever may be necessary to bring about the changes you want to make. Everything you do costs something. Education or self-improvement can only be done at the sacrifice of money or time on some things you might consider more pleasant or more fun. By the same token, spending time and money on those things you want to do for pleasure means that you may sacrifice education or other self-improvement that could mean better career opportunities and higher self-esteem.

In addition to being willing to make the necessary sacrifices, you must also be willing to change your attitudes toward yourself. When you wrote that you were not good at doing something or that you were uncomfortable in certain situations, you were showing that your attitude toward yoursekf in those areas was poor.

Chapter 5

WHAT HAVE I LEARNED, AND WHERE DO WE GO FROM HERE

In the first four chapters we learned:
1. What self-esteem is.
2. The four conditions that must exist for a person to have high self-esteem.
3. How we reach our level of self-esteem.
4. That a supervisor's actions can either positively or negatively affect an employee's self-esteem.
5. How to examine the factors that affect our own self-esteem.
6. That we must accept many of our feelings about ourselves.
7. That we can change or improve ourselves if our desire is great enough and we are willing to make sacrifices necessary to make those changes.
8. That self-esteem can be fragile and can be damaged by insensitive words or actions of another.

What must we now learn that will relate what has been covered in the first four chapters to people who work under our supervision?

The most important thing we must now learn is that every person has both strengths and weaknesses that combine to make up their level of self-esteem. They have skills, talents, abilities they feel good about, and they have things they don't like about themselves that they might want to improve or change.

While their strengths and weaknesses are not the same as yours, they too would have both RED entries and BLUE entries if they prepared a sheet as you did. Like you, their performance on the job is influenced by their internally identified strengths and weaknesses. Just as you will do your best work when you are called on to do a job that involves your RED entries, your subordinates will turn out better work on tasks that make use of their RED areas. They may not perform well—or even avoid—tasks that challenge them to use traits they would label BLUE.

The better acquainted you become with your employees the easier it will become for you to recognize their RED areas and their BLUE areas. This will help you in two ways: 1. It will help you determine which employee will be best suited for a particular type of task. This will result in better performance on the part of individual employees, which results in better performance by the group. 2. It will help you identify individual employee training needs or find areas in which they may simply need encouragement to try new things and develop self-confidence. The second thing you should learn is that a supervisor has two primary responsibilities:

1. To oversee the work assigned and insure that it is carried out as effectively, efficiently, and as accurately as possible within the guidelines of the organization.

2. To treat your subordinates as equals who are motivated toward success, personal satisfaction, and the goals of the organization the same as you are ...as long as you serve as their role model, mentor, cheerleader, helper, confidant, and disciplinarian—in short—their LEADER.

A supervisor cannot become the leader without understanding how his words and actions can either enhance a worker's self-esteem, injure her self-esteem, or leave it unaffected with neither negative nor positive consequences. The secret is knowing how to carry out the duties of the supervisor in the most positive manner. In the following chapters we will cover tasks the supervisor must routinely perform and determine how they can be done in ways that least challenge the worker's self-esteem. We will look at such things as interviewing and selecting new employees, the first day on the job, training, communication, performance appraisal, and leadership.

Chapter 6

FINDING THE NEW EMPLOYEE

There is only one reason to hire a new employee. That is because the organization needs the talent, skills and experience that will become available to help it fulfill its mission and reach its goals. In other words, it <u>needs</u> that person.

It should be safe to assume that if that person weren't needed you wouldn't be willing to expend the effort, time and money to find him. Thus, the managers and supervisors in your organization should make every effort to treat that person as a potential valuable asset to the organization from the time he applies for the job.

It doesn't matter if you are looking for a janitor, a high level manager or a technical employee, the same attitudes and atmosphere should prevail. From your first contact with a potential employee, he should be treated as a person who will be valuable to the business.

Too often we hear employees referred to as "just a janitor" or "just a secretary". But we don't hear engineers referred to as "just an engineer" or a manager as "just a manager". So why do some refer to the people they depend on to keep the premises clean and sanitary and free of dust that might interfere with the operation of sensitive piece of electronic equipment as "just a janitor"?

And why do some refer to those who are often the public's first contact with their business, who type their flawless correspondence, juggle their appointment schedules and perform a myriad of other duties ...sometimes personal... as "just a secretary"?

These employees, along with stock clerks, mailroom personnel, warehouse workers, bookkeepers and company vice presidents are all vital to the successful operation of the business. If not, they should not be on the payroll.

The content of an advertisement for a new employee is very important. It should describe the position to the extent that anyone applying feels that it is an important position and that the business realizes that it is important.

An ad containing only the word JANITOR and a telephone number will not attract applicants with the same experience and interest as an ad with a brief description of the work, the name of the company and some of the benefits that will be offered to the employee. The few additional dollars that will be spent on the ad will be repaid many times over by the quality of the applicants who will be attracted.

You may feel that all you need in a janitor is somebody who can sweep the floor and take out the trash, but what if a better ad would attract a young person who was satisfied to start as a janitor with your company while taking college courses at night? Those courses might lead him to a better position in the business. If he is not content to stay a janitor but wants to improve himself and sees opportunity within the business, his sweeping and taking out trash becomes more than "just a janitor." It becomes an opportunity to grow.

If an applicant knows that he is applying for an important position he will feel good about the organization and, in turn, better about himself. His self-esteem will be enhanced because he will feel that he is good enough to be considered for an important position in an important business.

Even if a candidate applies for a position after an announcement is closed and a person has been hired, he should still be treated with respect and as a potential employee. A curt, "Sorry, that job has been filled, you're too late", is not appropriate. You may think that you have no obligation to protect his self-esteem because he is not yet your employee. But neither do you have a right to damage that person's self-esteem.

Instead, it is better to tell the person that that position has been filled but you will be happy to accept his application and consider it for future openings.

You may respond that you do not have the space or time to keep all applications on file for some position that may never be available. Consider this possibility. Have someone screen applications that are received when you do not have an opening and retain only those that show that the applicant has some skills and talent that the business may need in the future. If the screener sees that the applicant has no particular potential to offer the business, discard the application. The application has been screened and the person has been considered.

Take time to quickly review this file of "potentials" when positions do come open.

You have made contact with a possible candidate and allowed him to retain his self-esteem. Your business will derive good public relations benefits from this approach. Especially if that applicant receives a call weeks or months later asking if he is still interested in working for you.

After you have received applications, reviewed them and selected candidates for interview, the next step is the most important in the selection process... the interview. Most applicants are uncomfortable when being interviewed for a job so this is the supervisor's first opportunity to put the applicant at ease.

Call the applicant by name. Hearing his name makes a person feel important and helps boost his self-esteem.

Describe the duties of the position and its importance. Tell the applicant how the work relates to the product or service supplied by the business. This is an important part of the interview. It lets the applicant understand that the position being filled is an important one and that the person selected will be valued because of the importance of the work to the operation of the business. "Just a janitor" should even be told how the job is important in terms of how cleanliness or lack of cleanliness affects the effectiveness of the business.

The interviewer must be interested in the applicant and show that interest. If the preliminary screening of applicants indicated that the person was a viable candidate but you find early in the interview that she is not acceptable, you can still show interest and let the candidate leave feeling that she has been considered. While you should not be expected to carry out as long an interview as you would for an applicant with a great deal of potential, you should make the interview long enough to let her retain a feeling of self worth and good self-esteem.

Many years ago I applied for a position with a government agency that is known for its state-of-the-art engineering. I drove five hundred miles for the interview that had been arranged several weeks before. When I got to the office the boss couldn't be found. I waited an hour past the scheduled time before the boss's assistant sighed, shrugged his shoulders and said that he guessed that he would have to talk to me.

He sat with his chair pushed back and his elbows resting on the edge of the desk ...practically lying on it. He played with a paper clip and never looked at me during the "interview". He hastily described the position in vague, general terms and asked me if I had any questions. After asking two or three and getting answers that were just as vague, I gave up. The "interview" lasted about ten minutes and I was glad when it was over.

When I left, I felt that the position was not considered very important and that the person who filled the vacancy would not be considered very important. My interest in the position was reduced to zero and my self-esteem was bruised. Fortunately, my feelings were soothed and my injured self-esteem boosted by the interest and enthusiasm shown by two other people who interviewed me for different positions later that day.

I relate this experience only as a bad example of how to conduct an interview. A person who has been subjected to that type of treatment will leave with a very poor image of the organization and a rather shaky self-esteem.

Too often a job interview is conducted in a way that leaves the impression that an interview is a unilateral task, and that the sole purpose is for the person being interviewed to sell the interviewer on selecting her for a vacancy.

An interview is, in reality, a buying and selling act on the part of both the interviewee and the interviewer. The person being interviewed is selling himself by presenting his education, experience, skills, talents, abilities and potential in hope of convincing you that he is the best "buy" for your business, much the same as a salesman would pitch his piece of equipment as the best for you.

You, as the interviewer, are hoping to "buy" the best person for the job. But you are also selling your business as the best "buy" for the person who may be investing his time, effort, past and future in your business.

As part of this "selling" of the business to the applicant, tell her about working conditions, some of the more important rules of the organization and the benefits that will become available to the person who is selected for the job. This gives the candidate information that will help her decide if this is the job she wants and the business she wants to work for, it also tells the employee that she is a viable candidate and that you consider her important enough to spend time telling her these important points. Besides, nobody likes to be surprised with important rules and regulations only after accepting a job and reporting for work.

Don't do all the talking. Give the candidate a chance to express herself and tell you things that she feels are important about herself—things that she feels are pertinent.

Most important, give the applicant time to say, "I'm sorry, I don't believe that the position you are describing is the position I want. Thank you for your time."

If the candidate says something like that and leaves, don't let your self-esteem be damaged or feel that a person had to be stupid not to want to work for you and your business. It is all right if the job was not what she wanted, and it is all right for her to tell you so.

After all, your advertisement may not have described the position accurately or you may not have done a very good job selling the job, yourself or the business.

An applicant should never leave the interview with the feeling that he has had the door to the business slammed behind him. The applicant can leave with self-esteem intact if told that you appreciate his interest in the position and the business, that a selection will be made in a short time and that she will hear from you whatever the decision.

While a telephone call may be the first notice to the applicant that she has been accepted for a job, a short letter should follow to make the acceptance "official".

For those applicants who weren't selected, follow up the interview with a short letter—even a form letter. Thank the applicant for his interest, time and effort. You don't have to tell him who was selected, only that he was not selected for that particular position. Invite him to apply for other positions that come open in the organization in the future. This helps him retain his self-esteem instead of having a feeling of rejection because he was not selected for that position.

This type letter serves several purposes. It serves as a formal closure for the applicant so far as that position is concerned; it results in good public relations and, if written correctly, leaves the applicant with self-esteem undamaged.

Don't forget those applicants who were not interviewed because you did not feel they were viable candidates. Send each of them a short letter thanking them for their interest but that they were not one of the best qualified. Invite them to apply for other positions. The applicant isn't left with a feeling of having been ignored or not considered important enough for a simple response. His self-esteem is left intact and, again, you benefit from the good public relations that result.

A friend applied for an advertised position of instructor in basic management at a local community college. He had a degree in management from a large state university and many years experience in management positions. He had numerous awards for his work and had taught supervisory development courses. He hand-delivered his application and a resume' to the college human resources office and waited, and waited, and waited. Nothing—not even a response thanking him for his application. His self-esteem survived with only minimal damage, but his attitude toward the college declined dramatically.

In terms of self-esteem, the interview should do several things:

1. Let applicants know that the position is important to the business and that the person who is selected will be important to the business.

2. Let the applicant know that you are interested in him as an individual.

3. Provide information that the applicant can use to decide whether or not she wants to work for you and the organization.

The applicant has a right to be able to decide whether or not she would not be able to retain her good self-esteem if she worked for you or the organization.

While that statement may seem to degrade you and your organization, the applicant does have the right to evaluate the position, you and the organization in those terms. At some time you have likely been exposed to a position, a boss or an organization that you would never consider working for. You probably felt that it would negatively affect the way people would evaluate you and that your feeling of self-worth would be damaged if you were in such a position or you worked for such a boss or in such an organization. Though you may not wish it so, an applicant has the right to evaluate the position, you and your organization in the same way.

4. Leave the selected applicant with a feeling of pride for having been selected for the position and a feeling of anticipation toward doing the work, working for you and being a part of the organization.

5. Leave those candidates who were not selected not with a feeling of rejection but with a feeling of satisfaction in having competed for an important position in an important business.

6. Last, but far from least, it should result in your having selected the best available candidate for the position.

It should leave you with a good feeling about yourself because you have presented the position, the business and yourself in the most accurate and the most positive manner.

How does the material covered in this chapter relate to the material we have already covered?

In the first chapter we learned that there are four conditions that must exist for a person to have high self-esteem:

SENSE OF CONNECTIVENESS
SENSE OF POWER OR CONTROL
SENSE OF UNIQUENES
SENSE OF ROLE MODELS

What have you done during the interview process to help the people interviewed increase or reinforce these four conditions?

If you have handled the interview well, the people you interviewed should leave with a sense of connectiveness or belonging because they have felt a part of the organization because you have made them feel that they are important enough to be considered for a position that would make them a permanent part of the organization. They have had an experience with your organization that they should be able to look back on as warm, friendly and rewarding ...even if they weren't hired.

During the interview the applicant should have had the feeling that you and he were equally in charge of the interview. He should have felt that he could ask questions of you, have time to answer your questions without being hurried and have the right to decline the job if he so desired. This would help him feel a sense of power or control.

During the interview you should have recognized the experience, training, skills, education that were his and his alone and acknowledged those individual characteristics to him. This, of course, would reinforce his sense of uniqueness.

Your demeanor during the interview should certainly have provided an example of the type employee that is valued by your organization. You should have provided a sense of role models.

It is very important that you get the best available candidate for the position, but what is next? What happens when that person walks in the door on her first day on the job?

In chapter seven we will look at an employee's most important day on the job... his first day on the job

Chapter 7

HERE I AM... WHAT NOW...??

Nearly everybody has some qualms about reporting for a new job. The actions of the supervisor can help calm the nervous butterflies in the stomach of the new employee or they can change a day of excited, pleasant anticipation into a traumatic experience.

The first day on a new job can be either a self-esteem building experience or one that can leave a new employee confused, in doubt of his ability to perform in the new position and deeply concerned as to whether or not he made the right decision when he decided to go to work for you.

Recently, I tutored a young lady who expressed an ardent desire to have a college education. She was twenty-six years old, married and had three small children. I found her to be bright, creative and full of desire to learn. She was one of those unfortunates who graduate from high school without mastering basic reading and writing skills. It was truly a sign of her intelligence that she realized that she had to work on self-improvement before she could attempt even remedial college courses.

When we first started working together on her reading and writing she had low self-esteem and was filled with doubt that she could "back up to the sixth grade and learn grammar and punctuation and all that other stuff." After only a few months she was writing original stories and critiques of P.B.S. programs such as a series on the mind. She blossomed and felt good about herself and her potential for the first time. Then she decided that she needed a part-time job to offset the expense of classes at the local community college.

````
`````

She applied at a local supermarket and was accepted. When she reported for her first day on her first job the manager handed her two videotapes and a loose-leaf binder "training manual" with mended, stained pages. She told the manager that she didn't have a VCR and was told that was her problem.

When she started to look for a place to sit down and read the "training manual" the manager told her that she was to study it on her own time and to do whatever a young stock clerk told her to do. Twice she asked the clerk questions and got only vague answers. The third time, she went to the manager for an answer. The manager slammed her pencil down on her desk, sighed, and asked, "What now?"

It was a sharp response in a "don't-bother-me" tone of voice. My young friend got the "training manual" and the videotapes and took them to the manager. She told the manager that she didn't think she could work there and left, self-esteem damaged and believing that she would never hold down a job. Later, as we talked about the incident, she realized that if she had not started our tutorial program that her low self-esteem would not have let her believe that she could get a job. She laughed and said that if she had managed to get a job she probably wouldn't have been able to ask questions, let alone walk into the manager's office and quit the way she had.

This is an extreme but true example of how bad the first day on a new job can be. It also shows how a little time helping a person can have a significant effect on that person's self-esteem.

Put yourself in the position of the young lady. Your self-esteem has been low and your reading and writing skills have been so poor that you refuse to write to friends or relatives. Just after you start improving those skills you apply for an entry-level job and your first day is a disaster. Imagine how you would feel if your first job, first day experience had been like hers.

Now ask yourself how her experience compares with the experience a new employee has on her first day in your organization. Think about how the new employee is welcomed into the organization. Is she helped through the first day jitters or thrown into the job with little or no indoctrination? Is she introduced to others with whom she will be working in the organization? Is she faced with information overload as soon as she reports for work? Each organization is different in work situations, but no matter what kind of work you are involved in, it is vital that you make the new employee feel a part of your organization from the beginning and that at the end of the first day she looks forward to the second day with a feeling of eager anticipation rather than a feeling of dread or uncertainty. One of the most important needs of a new employee is the need for information... information that she needs to start work with a feeling of confidence. The information she needs is in addition to what she will be given in a formal training program. This is information that she needs to know about rules, regulations, her coworkers, and the workplace. I recommend that you make a list of the vital points you need to cover so that you will not forget anything that the new employee needs to know.

Before a new employee comes on board make up a list of things you need to tell a worker on the first hour of the first day. Put yourself in the position of wearing two hats, that of the supervisor and that of the new employee. Try to think of the things you would like to know if you were new on the job. Then think of all the things that the new employee needs to know from the standpoint of the supervisor.

Put the things you think of in writing and then put them in a logical sequence. Put the general bits of information first; hours of work, lunch periods, break periods, rules on absences, location of break and lunch areas, holidays, rotation of lunch and break periods so that the work area is never unmanned, and, oh yes, one thing that is often forgotten or avoided because the new employee is of the opposite sex... the location of the restroom.

Next, list those items that are more directly related to the position; how the work fits into the overall objectives of the organization, performance standards, anything that you can think of that the new employee needs to know in order to begin work with confidence. If you run dry and can't think of things, just ask the people who work for you... especially the newer employees. They are the ones who can best remember their first day in the organization. Don't hesitate to ask your workers for advice, they are your best source of information on the subject. Besides, your asking them for help will make them feel good about themselves and about you. It shows that you value their judgment and that you aren't one of those supervisors who believe that they have all the answers.

When you ask them for things to include in your list, also ask about things that were covered their first day that would have been better held until later... when they were more familiar with the organization and the work.

When the new worker reports for work, keep your list handy for reference and to assure that you do not miss some important information that will help the new worker.

You may feel that this is a lot of work to go through for a new employee, but remember that the well-informed employee is the employee who will fit into the organization the quickest. Also, the new employee you are expecting will probably not be the last new employee you will have. Keep this list for future use and keep editing it to assure that it is up to date.

A word of caution. Don't put information on this "first day-first hour" list that would be more appropriate or will be covered in a formal training program such as the details of work procedures. This is a first day information list, not a training device. If possible, meet the new employee when she reports for work. In larger organizations the new employee may report to the Personnel Office (or in the current vernacular, The Human Resources Office) for a general briefing that is given to all new employees when they report for work. In a small organization, on the other hand, a new employee may simply tell a secretary or receptionist that she is reporting for work and the secretary or receptionist will either take the new worker to her work area or call for someone to come and get her. If this is the case in your organization the "first hour-first day" list is especially important because you are responsible for giving the new employee all the information she needs to know that first day.

If you, her supervisor, can't be available because of an important meeting or some other valid reason, be sure that you assign a knowledgeable employee to greet the new worker. Don't let the new employee report to her work place and then sit and twiddle her fingers while she waits for you. Give the employee you assign to meet the new employee a briefing on what you want her to cover from your "first hour-first day" list. Then take over as soon as you can.

From the beginning, let the new worker know that she is important to you and to the organization and its goals. Again, it doesn't matter if the new employee is an engineer, a secretary or a janitor; that person's work is important so the person is important. Let the person know it.

After you cover the items on your "first hour-first day" list take the new worker to the specific area where she will work. Introduce her to her coworkers. Tell her how her work interfaces with the others. In an office situation tell her where supplies are kept and how to get them. If you have a "lead" employee in the organization, this is the time to turn the new employee over to her for more specific information on the job. Be sure that the "lead" understands the importance of proper attitude toward the new worker. The "lead" must understand that the first day is the most important day on a new job because the new worker's experience on that day has a great bearing on her attitude toward the organization.

We all know that first impressions are important. They are just as important in work situations as in social situations and the new employee's first impression of the organization is fully as important as the first impression of a potential customer or client.

Some supervisors may feel that the kind of new employee greeting that I have outlined amounts to "coddling" the employee, but it is far from it. It only amounts to getting off on the right foot with a new employee by making her comfortable in a new situation and assuring that she has information she needs to start her work.

Other supervisors may believe that this type greeting doesn't apply because of the type of work done by the organization, but a carpenter or a brick mason needs to know the policies of the organization, whom he will be working with, overtime policies, when he will be paid, etc. just as much as the office worker. He also needs to know the quality work you expect. He should be given an overall picture of the work that the business is doing and the role his job plays in meeting the goals of the organization. He should have the feeling that he is not just driving nails or laying brick, rather that he is carrying out an important task involved in constructing a building or a home.

All employees need information. One of the most common failings of supervisors or managers is the failure to communicate downward in the organization while demanding that employees tell management everything that happens. If a supervisor fails to give needed information to a new employee, that new employee is probably justified in feeling that this failure to communicate vital information will continue.

What does the employee gain in terms of self-esteem

enhancement from a first day on the job that is an informative, welcoming day combined with a day of first work experience?

Let's again review the four conditions that must exist for a person to have high self-esteem and what a supervisor can do to help the new employee feel that she has met these four conditions in the work area.

A SENSE OF CONNECTIVENESS.

A sense of connectiveness is a sense of belonging or being connected to a group or other person. The supervisor can help the new employee have this sense of belonging by assuring that the employee is made aware from the beginning that she is important to the performance of the work of the organization and not that she has to earn a spot to be a part of the inner clique of the business. She is a part of the business because she is there and ready to do her best.

A SENSE OF POWER, CONTROL.

In some work situations it may be difficult, but not impossible, to help the new employee feel this sense of power or control. It can be as easy as giving the employee responsibility for making certain decisions in connection with her work or by telling her that she is responsible for her own quality control of her work. An important method is to invite the employee to make suggestions for improving work methods or improving the product as she learns her new job... and assuring her that you will honestly consider any suggestions. Never assume that because an employee is new to your business that she doesn't have knowledge or experience that can be very valuable to your business.

A SENSE OF UNIQUENESS.

When the supervisor talks with the new employee on the first day he should assure the worker that the unique talents, skills, knowledge that the employee has are recognized and will be valuable to the organization. The supervisor can reinforce this sense by saying something like "Your experience in public relations and your training in writing were especially important in our selecting you for this position. That background will be very helpful in this job and can make you a viable candidate for advancement within the company." This lets her know that you are aware of her unique combination of skills and experience and, that because of these factors, she has some degree of control over her future with the organization.

A SENSE OF ROLE MODELS.

The behavior of the supervisor on the employee's first day gives her the first clue as to the type behavior that is acceptable to the organization. If the supervisor is cordial yet businesslike, this tells the employee that this is the way the business operates and the manner in which she should carry out her work. If the supervisor lets her sit and wait while he chats with someone else, gives her a half hearted indoctrination or says a quick hello and shoves her off on an unprepared, busy employee to tell her some of the things she needs to know, the message to the new employee is that lack of concern for employees; i.e. sloppy, incomplete work and little concern for details is an acceptable way to perform.

As you prepare your "first day-first hour" checklist, consider how the information you give the new employee and your attitudes and performance on that first day will affect the new person. Think of how you can help the new person by providing for the four conditions that must exist for a person to have high self-esteem. Make the first hour of the first day work for the new employee, for you and for the organization.

Now that the new employee is on board, knows the basics about the organization and the job and yes, even where the restroom is located, let's talk about training. Let's talk about why it is important to both the employee and the business and the things that are imperative if your training program is to be successful.

Chapter 8
TELL ME WHAT TO DO AND HOW TO DO IT

Now that you have your new employee on board, the next step is to give that employee the training needed to perform the job in a manner that meets the standards of the organization. Some employers believe that organized, formal training is too time consuming and too costly. They fail to realize that the cost of a well-planned, complete training program can actually be cost saving in terms of better product or service from the time the employee starts doing the work.

Other employers think of training only in terms of how it will benefit the business without considering the needs of the employee. A common ailment in the business world is the extensive, intensive ten-minute training program—"Be at work at eight, work till five, an hour for lunch, the restroom is at the end of the hall, here's the work, do it."

An effective training program certainly should be designed around the needs of the organization, but it must also be designed around the needs of the employee.

RICHARDSON'S FIRST LAW OF EFFECTIVE TRAINING:
Effective training must fulfill two important needs:
(Of course it's my law—it's my book!)

1. COMPETENCE

Competence means that the employee learns the basic skills and procedures for doing the job that he was hired to do. Competence has to do with ability to do the work. The American Heritage Dictionary defines competence as, "Properly or well qualified; capable," and, "Adequate for the purpose; suitable, sufficient." A combination of good selection and adequate training content should produce an employee who is competent—one who is physically and mentally capable of doing the job, and who is familiar with the tools, forms, procedures, and both quality and performance standards necessary to do the job.

2. CONFIDENCE

Unless training is structured so that the new employee gains confidence—the feeling of assurance or certainty that he is mentally, physically, and emotionally able to do the work—the training has been only minimally successful. Competence is not enough. The employee must have little or no doubt that he is ready and able to go to work when the initial training is completed.

How do we structure training that gives the employee both the competence and the confidence to provide the business with the product or service desired? There are three basic methods of training:

1. Tell
2. Tell and Show
3. Tell—Show—Let Do.

TELL

All of us have had, at some time, a teacher or instructor who felt that the way to teach was to stand in front of the class and talk, and talk, and talk. College professors are notorious for using this "Tell" method of teaching. This method may be appropriate for teaching some subjects, but unless the teacher has an exceptional ability to hold the students' attention and inspire them to learn, the students' minds will begin to wander. Telling is the least effective way to train or educate because it involves only one of our five senses (seeing, hearing, touching, smelling, tasting). The more of these senses that are involved in learning, the more successful the training is likely to be. A person's ability to remember is enhanced as a greater number of the senses are involved.

TELL AND SHOW

The "Tell and Show" method of instructing has a definite advantage over the "Tell" method because it incorporates the use of more than one of our five senses. The "Show" part of this type of instruction may be anything from movies or videotapes to actually showing the work process. Instead of simply telling the trainee about certain tools, forms, parts, machines, materials, and processes that will be used on the job, the instructor shows them to the trainees and demonstrates them in use.

TELL, SHOW, LET DO

The best training method is the "Tell, Show and Let Do" method. Under this method, the instructor tells what to do and how to do it; shows and demonstrates the tools, materials, and processes; and lets the trainee practice doing the job in a simulated work situation. This lets the instructor evaluate the effectiveness of the training and determine how much the trainee has learned in each area of instruction. The instructor can also find out if the trainee needs reinforcement on any part of the training.

Equally important, it gives the trainee an opportunity to get a feel for the work, to show what she has learned, and to satisfy herself that she has the competence and the confidence to do the work before she is put into a position where production and quality are evaluated. This method also gives the business an opportunity to weed out trainees who are not suited for the work, and the trainee a chance to determine whether or not the job is right for her.

Why is the third method the most effective of the three? It uses more of the trainee's senses. The first uses only the sense of hearing. The second—"Tell and Show"—uses two of the trainee's senses—hearing and seeing. The "Tell, Show, and Let Do" method involves hearing, seeing, and touching. The touching may involve any number of tactile (touching) sensations (the texture of the material; the weight of the tools; finger, hand, arm, body movement or position, etc.). The other two senses—smell and taste—may also be called upon in some situations. Could you imagine a potential cook going through a training session in which he was not given an opportunity to taste or smell the food? In some cases, an employee may have to identify different materials or products by their odor.

RICHARDSON'S SECOND LAW OF EFFECTIVE TRAINING:

Effective training involves as many of the employee's five senses as is practical.

Training must be designed so that it gives the trainee an opportunity to use as many of the five senses as possible. The more that are used, the better the employee's attention will be kept, and the more the employee will retain.

If you are a parent, or you have ever worked with children, you know that you can only show a child how to do something a few times before the child wants to try to do it himself. This, I believe, indicates clearly that the best, fastest, and most natural way of learning is by doing.

While it may be difficult to use this method in some situations because of the expense of duplicating the actual work situation for training purposes, it is the best for providing the trainee both competence and confidence to begin a job.

But effective training for the new employee must cover more than how to do the job. Good training should also answer the question of "WHY?" Why do we do this job? Why is it important to the organization? It should show the trainee how the work done on her job fits into the product or service furnished by the organization.

The training discussed to this point is commonly referred to as vestibule training, or training provided upon the employee's entry into a new position, but what about training after the employee is on the job?

Training is a continuing process. Any time a supervisor shows an employee that she has made a mistake and shows or tells the employee how to correct it and avoid making it again, the supervisor is training that employee. If materials are changed, procedures are updated, new products are introduced, or if the employee is assigned additional work, new training is required.

If an employee is not meeting work standards, additional training should be given before adverse action is taken. A little reinforcement in the form of remedial training may improve the employee's work and save the expense and the time involved in hiring and training a new employee.

There are, of course, some factors that should be considered when providing training for an employee:

FIRST, the training should be pertinent. In other words, the training should be usable by the employee in her present position or should prepare that employee for new work. Sometimes, employees are sent to training programs that are held at attractive locations such as a resort area—as nothing more than recognition of good work. When travel, lodging, tuition and time lost from the job are considered, it can be a very expensive way to reward good performance. The employee might rather have recognition in the form of money or even training that might enhance his opportunity for advancement.

SECOND, management must accept the training. For example, if an employee is sent to a training course on clear writing and management requires correspondence and reports to be written in third person or in heavy legalese or esoteric jargon, the employee will know that her time has been wasted and that the training was meaningless because management does not actually accept the training.

THIRD, the training must be productive. It must be

planned and conducted so that the employee knows that she has gained something of value for her time and effort.

In order to assure the employee will complete the training with both the competence and the confidence to do the job, the training must use as many of the person's five senses as possible, and it must be pertinent, productive, and accepted by management. But there is another factor that must be present: the training must be self-esteem enhancing. The training style must be supportive. The training must concentrate on enhancing the person's skills and knowledge. It should recognize progress and successes and should not concentrate on the errors that trainees make during the learning phase. Errors should be recognized as a part of the learning process. They should be corrected in a non-challenging way that does not reflect on the trainee's intelligence or value as a person.

Good training is one of the ways a supervisor can build employees' self-esteem. How does it build on the four conditions that are needed for a person to have high self-esteem?

SENSE OF CONNECTIVENESS

A complete, effective training program for a new employee tells the employee that she is a part of the organization from the beginning. It tells her that she is valuable enough that the organization is willing to invest time and money to assure that she will be competent and will feel confident in her ability to perform the duties of the job. From the beginning, she will be able to say, "I am a part of this organization."

A SENSE OF POWER—CONTROL

With a person's feelings of competence and confidence comes a sense of power. "I have the ability and the skills to do this job and do it well. The training that I received provided me with skills that many others do not have. By demonstrating what I have learned and showing that I can perform well, I have a sense of a degree of control over my work and my future."

A SENSE OF UNIQUENESS

An effective manager or supervisor recognizes the strengths of an employee and provides training that will give the employee an opportunity to use his unique skills. By doing this, the supervisor assures the employee that he recognizes the employee as an individual and verifies this by informing the employee that she has special skills or talents that are worth developing.

ROLEMODELS

A supervisor is in the best position to give the employee a sense of having a good role model when serving as an instructor or giving any type of on-the-job training. As the supervisor gives the training, he can also model the enthusiasm and interest in the work that he expects from the employee.

Next, let's look at the communication process and the positive effect that good communication in the workplace can have on an employee's self-esteem.

Chapter 9

TALK WITH ME...NOT TO ME

Poor communication has been blamed for many of the ills in our society today: failure of relationships, problems with our children, interracial misunderstandings, and even work relationships between supervisor and employee. Often, the communication problem between supervisor and employee is that there is little or no communication either downward or upward in the organization. When there is little communication downward through the organization it is because management believes that the workers need only the minimum of information required to do their jobs. Beyond that, managers often believe that workers already know, workers don't need to know, or workers don't want to know what is going on in the organization, even when it directly affects the workers.

NOTE: When you read the terms "upward in the organization," or "downward in the organization, these words are used only in terms of the normally accepted organization chart format. It does not, in any way, imply higher or lower in terms of ability, intelligence, or importance to the organization.

FLOW OF INFORMATION

When information flows in only one direction—downward—only half of the communication process is completed.

Direction, evaluation, planning, and goals—nearly all communication flows from the top of the organization downward to the person who performs the work of the organization, with little opportunity for any upward communication. Suggestions for improving production, comments, and ideas for markets or products rarely make their way from the bottom of the organization to the top.

What does this lack of a channel for upward communication say to the employee? It says that we (management) do not believe that you (the worker) have anything of value to offer the organization in the way of original, creative, intelligent thought. If we ever want your ideas, we will solicit them by way of our normal, one-way, downward communication system—but don't hold your breath.

What is the effect of this attitude on employee self-esteem? The message becomes clear: "If my ideas, thoughts and opinions are not good enough for this organization, I must not be very valuable to this organization—maybe not to any organization, or to anybody."

THE COMMUNICATION PROCESS

The easiest way to understand communication and how problems arise is to look at a graphic illustration of the communication process. Communication is a process because it consists of several steps or activities. For this illustration, let's assume that the communication takes place between Sam (the supervisor) and Sally.

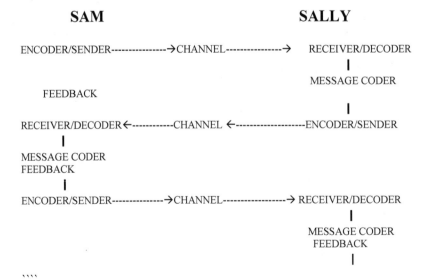

RECEIVER/DECODER ←----------CHANNEL←-------------------ENCODER/SENDER
|
(CONTINUE)

In the first step we refer to the person sending the message (Sam) as the ENCODER and SENDER because he starts the process by putting the message into the format, words, terms, acronyms, language, symbols that he feels appropriate. He crafts the message in his personal "code" using his own language, terms, etc., based on his knowledge of the subject, his knowledge of the language, even his ethnic and social background. To him, the message he sends seems clear and appropriate. Sam then sends the message on its way, using the channel he feels appropriate. The channel may be telephone, email, memo, letter, fax, radio, face-to-face oral, or any other method of transmitting information.

The person at the other end of the channel (Sally) is called the RECEIVER/DECODER because she not only receives the message but also is required to decode the sender's message to make it meaningful to her. In this decoding step Sally interprets what Sam has sent by using her own knowledge of the subject, her own knowledge of the language, her own ethnic and social background, all of which may be far different from Sam's.

Next comes the process of Sally encoding a message back to Sam that indicates her understanding of the original message and any additional information she might want to relay. This step is called FEEDBACK because it feeds back to Sam information on how well his message has been received and interpreted. Sally, now the ENCODER in the FEEDBACK step, uses her own language, terms, words, to say to the original sender, "This is my understanding of the message you sent."

Now, Sam, the original ENCODER/SENDER, becomes the RECEIVER/ DECODER of the returning message or FEEDBACK. He decodes Sally's message in terms of his own knowledge, language, and background.

````
````

Sam's reply, like Sally's in the preceding step, may contain both FEEDBACK on his understanding of the message received and some additional MESSAGE—again in his own code or words.

In the ideal communication situation, the process will continue until there is agreement on the intent of the message on the part of those involved. This, of course, assumes that each party feels free to communicate openly with the other; there is no intimidation or self-esteem problem that limits one person's ability to carry out his or her half of the process.

PROBLEM AREAS

So where might we find problems that inhibit successful communication?

RICHARDSON'S FIRST LAW OF COMMUNICATION:
There is potential for a problem at any step in the communication process.

First, the message may be the wrong message. The idea might not have been thought through to insure that the message is necessary, timely, accurate, appropriate, and is being sent to the right person. A message can be affected by anger, depression, sadness, or even joy.

Second, the words used in the message (code) may not be appropriate for the receiver-decoder. Too much technical or legal jargon may be used. Words chosen might not have the same meaning to a person with a different ethnic or social background. Improper grammar or punctuation can be a problem that not only affects the meaning of the message, but also may reflect on the intelligence of the sender and distract the receiver who should be concentrating on the message. The encoding step becomes more complicated when we learn that the 500 most used words in the English language have more than fourteen thousand meanings depending on the way a word is used.

Third, the channel might not be the right one for the message. When legal points, numbers, or statistics are involved, or the message is formal in nature, the message should be in writing. If it is necessary that the message be oral, it should be followed up in writing as soon as possible as a form of verification.

When the message is straightforward, and a personal reaction and reply are wanted quickly, oral communication-- either face-to-face or by telephone—may be appropriate-- verified in writing if necessary. With the number of communication channels available to us today, (computers, fax, voice mail, etc.) the choices are many, but the channel should be carefully selected, considering both the type message and the receiver. Remember, even sky-writing, towed banners, signs, grunts, groans, shrugs, whistles, body language, facial expressions, are some of the many channels for communication. Choose the best one for the situation.

Fourth, the decoder-receiver can derive the wrong meaning from the message. In addition to dissimilar backgrounds being a problem, the attitude and emotions of the receiver can cause misinterpretation just as the attitude or emotions of the sender can cause an improper or inappropriate message to be sent.

Fifth, feedback might not be given or even requested. When there is no feedback, there is no assurance that the message received is the message intended to be sent.

RICHARDSON'S SECOND LAW OFCOMMUNICATION:
BE CERTAIN THAT YOUR MESSAGE IS THE RIGHT ONE, STRUCTURED CORRECTLY FOR THE RECEIVER/ DECODER, AT THE RIGHT TIME, USING THE RIGHT CHANNEL.

RICHARDSON'S THIRD LAW OF COMMUNICATION
GIVE FEEDBACK, ASK FOR & ACCEPT FEEDBACK.

Give feedback even when the person who sends you a

message does not request it. But it is important that feedback be asked for in a non-threatening way.

As an illustration, let's assume that you have just given a subordinate instructions on something you want done. How do you ask for feedback?

"0. K., now tell me what you heard so I'll be sure you understand what I want."

Or:

"O.K., I want to make sure I made myself clear and that I didn't leave anything out. So feedback what I said."

Which is better? The first says to the employee that she may not have been listening or might not be bright enough to understand what you said. This approach certainly does nothing to preserve the employee's self-esteem.

The second puts the onus on you to carry out your part of the communication correctly. It says that I want to be sure that what I said was clear and complete and understandable. It asks, did I do my job well? It asks for feedback without injuring the other person's self-esteem.

RICHARDSON'S FOURTH LAW OF COMMUNICATION
Encourage communication both upward and downward in the organization.

Be open to the needs, ideas, suggestions, hints, of the workers. They are the ones who do the work that results in the success or the failure of the organization. During my nearly four decades of work with government agencies—most of those years as a supervisor—I have seen several cases in which a taciturn employee opened up and made valuable, viable suggestions for improvements in work methods, work assignments, organization goals, or safety measures as the result of a new supervisor letting that worker know that the supervisor was open to, and encouraged, upward communication.

````
````

RICHARDSON'S FIFTH LAW OF COMMUNICATION:
Don't expect your employees to be mind readers.

A good example is the supervisor who sends half a message and expects the employee to understand the full, intended message. In one case I witnessed, a supervisor left a booklet with a short note attached on an employee's desk. The note read, "Sally, there seems to be some good information in this booklet. (Signed,) Sam."

A week later Sally was called into Sam's office. "Where is the report on that booklet I left on your desk?" Sam asked, a touch of anger in his tone.

Sally thought for a moment, and then remembered the booklet. "You just wrote that there was some good information in it. You didn't ask for a report."

Sam sighed and slumped in his chair. "You didn't even ask, did you?" he said.

Sally was not a mind reader. Don't expect your workers to be mind readers.

It is important that supervisors and managers realize that it is a compliment when workers feel free to relay their thoughts, ideas, and suggestions upward. It should make the supervisor or manager know that the workers trust him and that he is considered receptive to new ideas: earmarks of more than a supervisor, a leader. (A real self-esteem builder for the supervisor.)

BARRIERS TO EFFECTIVE COMMUNICATION:

We can improve communication within an organization only if we recognize some of the primary barriers to effective communication.

THE ORGANIZATION.

The formal structure of an organization can be one of the greatest barriers to good communication. Excessive layers of hierarchy create formal, structured lines of communication that distance workers from management. A message that has to pass through several levels before it reaches the intended receiver is more susceptible to distortion, being delayed or even stopped. People at lower levels have little or no opportunity to communicate with anyone more than one level above their own position.

ASSUMPTIONS.
"I thought you knew that; I did." "I didn't think you would be involved." "I assumed...." I thought..." "I thought I told you..."

How often have we heard these excuses? If a message concerns a person's job, his performance, his future, or his life, make sure that person gets that message personally, and gets it when he needs it. It is better that a person be told more than once than to assume that she has been told when she has not.

Even if the worker has received the message, it may have been received unofficially when it should have come to the employee through the official communication path (so, possibly not taken seriously), or even distorted as it tumbled through the rumor mill. The message received may not have been the one you wanted to send. Remember, the worker's self-esteem benefits when you take time to convey a message personally.

INFORMATION OVERLOAD.
Some people will not get information they need. The other side of the coin is that some people, especially managers and supervisors, may be overloaded with information. As a modern-day example—the computer is a wonderful tool, but overuse can be a by-product. When information is stored in a computer, there is potential for that same information to be returned in innumerable formats. This can result in a temptation to "need" more information than we can use and digest simply because it is available. Overload can also come from "shot gunning" correspondence throughout the organ-

ization. Make sure that the people who need to know do know, but don't burden others with information for which they have no valid need.

TIME PRESSURES.

Take time to insure that the message you are sending is the message you intended. Give time for feedback. Don't rush through important instructions and then become upset when the job is not done as you wanted. TAKE TIME, MAKE TIME to send the proper message. On the other hand, don't interrupt the boss to tell him something when he obviously does not have time to afford you the attention you and your message deserve. Make an appointment that is convenient for both of you.

Before we look at how good communication affects the self-esteem of everyone in the organization, let's explore the most overlooked communication channel available.

ORAL COMMUNICATION.

The cheapest, quickest, easiest, and most expressive communication is face-to-face oral communication. It is the most expressive for the same reason that "Tell, show, and do" is the best training method as discussed in chapter 8. Oral communication involves more than one of our senses. We not only hear the words the other person uses, we hear the way the words are spoken, the vocal inflection applied to each word, the speed—or urgency—of the words. We can also see the facial expressions and the body language of the speaker. Researchers tell us that 80% of oral communication is non-spoken, so it is important that the effective supervisor be aware of the expressions and body language, and what signals they may be sending in relation to the spoken message. The two may or may not be consistent. A careful listener hears more than words alone.

````
````

Oral communication applies the same basic steps as any other method: the sender forms the message, encodes it, and sends it. The receiver decodes the message. And this is where a most important step takes place.

LISTENING

In business, people spend approximately 10% of their time writing, 15% reading, 35% speaking, and 40% listening. These figures certainly point out the importance of good listening skills. A problem arises when we hear, but we don't listen. We may appear to be listening when we are merely hearing the sounds the speaker makes, not listening to what the speaker is saying.

The brain has a wonderful way of selecting what we hear. It weeds out extraneous noises and puts them into the background so that we are able to select only the sounds we want to hear. The brain also has a problem of thinking faster than a person can speak. This can result in our guessing what the speaker is going to say or our thinking too much about our reply while the other person is still talking. Our response may be irrelevant or non-responsive.

Don't assume that the responsibility for good oral communication rests on the speaker; equally important is the role of the receiver. To insure that we receive and decode the speaker's words correctly, and that our feedback is accurate and responsive, we must learn the skill of LISTENING.

HOW TO IMPROVE LISTENING:

1. LOOK AT THE SPEAKER. When you look directly at the speaker as she speaks, you let her know that you are attentive and sensitive to both her and her message. Wandering eyes give the message that neither the speaker nor what is being said is important enough to be given the listener's full attention.

2. RESPOND TO THE SPEAKER. As you look at the speaker indicate your interest and attentiveness by nodding or responding orally: "Uh huh," "I see," "Yes," "That is a good point," etc, or paraphrasing feedback to the speaker. As an example, here is another conversation between Sally and Sam:

"Sam, I'm afraid I can't do this work you gave me."

"Do you mean you can't do it because you don't know how?"

"It's not that. I mean that I can't take it seriously."

"You can't take it seriously because you don't think it's important?"

"I know that it is important, but the work I do is higher level and more difficult than this. I think somebody with less experience could handle it."

"You think it would be good training for a newer employee?"

"Well, yes, it would be good training. I'll show him how to do it if he needs help."

"You made a good point. I appreciate your offering to help train someone to do it. That would be good experience for you."

In this example Sam (who has obviously been paying attention) has used feedback designed to draw out Sally's thoughts on the matter. Although Sally has not expressed it, she feels that the work is below her experience level and position in the organization, and that to do the work would negatively affect her self-esteem. Being given the job of training the other employee means that Sam has recognized that she has the knowledge and ability to train another person, which gives Sally's self-esteem a boost. The newer, less experienced worker may find that being chosen for new work might enhance his self-esteem.

3. WORK AT LISTENING. Good listening skills involve some work. Poor listening is passive listening. Don't try to fake attention; it doesn't work. Good listeners are willing to expend the energy to understand the speaker.

4. OPEN YOUR MIND. Poor listeners may overly react to emotional words and jump to conclusions as to what the speaker is saying. Words in themselves do not carry meaning. Listen to the total message. The combinations of words and the way people express them bring significance to words.

5. USE THE SPEED OF YOUR BRAIN. People think many times faster than they speak. Good listeners use the gaps in the other's speech to mentally analyze and summarize what the speaker is saying.

6. USE LISTENING SKILLS TO GROW. Poor listeners tend to turn off their brain whenever they feel that what the other person is saying is over their heads. Good listeners listen even more attentively in order that they can ask questions and expand their knowledge.

The above six ways to improve listening skills combine as ACTIVE LISTENING. This involves more than just listening to words. It requires work letting the speaker know you are listening, and checking with the speaker through feedback to find out if you are REALLY understanding what he is saying.

Psychotherapist Carl Rogers first used the term "Active Listening" in the 1950s. Later, Psychologist Thomas Gordon popularized it in his book, L.E.T. Leadership Effectiveness Training. (Linver, 1978)

The last and most important part of learning good listening skills is to STOP TALKING. You cannot do a good job of listening if you don't STOP TALKING. There seems to be an internal connection—not yet discovered by scientists—that causes the ears to close off any incoming sounds whenever the mouth opens to emit sounds.

The question that must be answered in the context of this book is, how can good communication help improve employees' self-esteem; how does good communication help provide the four conditions that must be present for a person to have high self-esteem?

SENSE OF CONNECTIVENESS:

When a good communication system exists with information flowing freely both upward and downward, an employee is much more apt to have a feeling of being considered an integral part of the organization. When a supervisor or manager takes the time and makes an effort to listen to the ideas, suggestions, complaints, even personal matters of the employee, he helps the employee connect with the organization. That feeling of connectiveness stimulates pride in self, the work, and the organization.

SENSE OF POWER—CONTROL:

A communication system that provides an open upward channel for suggestions assures employees that their ideas on ways to improve the work process or the end product will be heard. When viable suggestions are approved and rewarded, employees have a sense of some power and control over their jobs and the way they do their work.

SENSE OF UNIQUENESS:

Blanket communication to employees in the form of procedures, office rules, and general announcements is necessary in any organization, but an employee's uniqueness can be recognized when one-to-one communication is in order. Recognize the employee's knowledge of the subject, his experiences, his need to know. Recognize that each worker is an individual and communicate with each as an individual. Such a seemingly small thing as addressing the person by name means that you recognize that person as an individual.

SENSE OF ROLE MODELS:

The way you communicate with your workers will be reflected in the way they communicate with you. If your style is open, your workers are more apt to feel free to communicate openly with you. Show them how you want them to communicate.

````
````

This chapter has concentrated on communication between you and your employees, but the subject cannot be closed without our looking at the type of communication that most affects our own self-esteem... *self communication.* In earlier chapters we discussed how our self-esteem is formed on the basis of our experiences, and how it is affected by what we say to ourselves about our looks, skills, talents, intelligence, and our ability to meet challenges. Self-doubt communicates failure; positive thoughts communicate success. As I said earlier in this chapter: *Self communication must always be positive.*

In the next chapter we will look at the performance appraisal process and how it can be done honestly without bashing the self-esteem of the employee whose work is less than exemplary.

Chapter10

HOW AM I DOING????

Performance appraisal in one form or another has certainly been with us ever since the first time someone worked under the supervision of another person. The building of the pyramids took an estimated twenty years and required more than one hundred thousand workers. One pyramid covers as much as thirteen acres and is constructed of nearly 2 million stone blocks weighing an average of 2 tons. An undertaking of that magnitude certainly involved planning, organizing, directing, and evaluating (four basic functions of management), and the evaluation function must have included the evaluation and appraisal of both the work and the workers. Surely there was some type record made of the work progress and whether or not each slave (literally) pulled his own weight. I hesitate to think of what the penalty might have been for those who didn't.

The beginning of our modern performance appraisal systems can be traced to Scotland in the early 1800's when Robert Owens, owner of New Lanark cotton mills, used character books and blocks to appraise his workers. Daily performance was recorded in the character books. Character blocks were placed at each workstation; the color of the block showed Owens' evaluation of the worker's worth to the organization. The blocks were visible to all workers, so everybody worked harder to merit the right color block.

While that may seem a rather harsh way to treat workers—with everyone's appraisal visible to all the other workers—Robert Owens was truly a social reformer of his day. He believed that people were more important than machines, and that they had to be treated properly for them to be productive. As an example: instead of hiring children as cheap labor, he hired adults and built schools for their children.

In 1813 the U.S. Army was the first organization in this country to establish a performance appraisal system, followed by a system for civilian government workers in 1842. Industry generally did not start programs until after World War I, and they were not widely accepted until after World War II.

RICHARDSON'S FIRST LAW OF PERFORMANCE APPRAISAL.

The supervisor does not appraise the employee as a human being. He appraises the employee's performance against a clear, previously established set of performance standards by which he appraises the performance of all employees who perform the same tasks.

PERFORMANCE APPRAISAL: ONCE A YEAR, OR EVERY DAY???

Is performance appraisal an unpleasant, once-a-year task in your organization? Is appraisal limited to a few check marks or hastily written, cryptic statements on a form signed by you and the employee? Do you really think so? Think again. Performance appraisal is a minute-by-minute, hour-by-hour, day-by-day part of supervision, even if the formal paperwork is completed only once or twice a year.

While the formal appraisal system is valuable to both the organization and the employee, of more importance to the employee is the supervisor's appraisal of his work each day. The formal, periodic rating may indicate that the employee's performance is good, but the supervisor's manner of dealing with her each day may deliver another message. Even if your formal appraisal might result in a performance award, your day-to-day treatment of that employee might well result in her wondering which is valid, your formal report, or your general attitude toward her and her work.

Inconsistency between the informal and the formal

appraisal can result in an employee who is confused and doubtful of her worth to the organization—and damaged self-esteem.

Immediacy is the key to appraising hour-to-hour, day-to-day work. If an employee finishes a piece of work and it is done properly and promptly, a simple, "good job," or "looks good" may be all you need to say, but it should be said immediately. Delaying this type acknowledgement reduces its effectiveness.

RICHARDSON'S SECOND LAW OF PERFORMANCE APPRAISAL
A few words of praise or a pat on the back on a regular basis does more to enhance an employee's self-esteem and performance than 364 days, seven hours of uncertainty and an hour of formal recognition.

By the same token, the supervisor should act on errors or omissions immediately, not hours or days later—unless there is a valid reason for waiting. Bring them to the employee's attention while the work is fresh in the worker's memory. This makes it easier for him to recall why or how he made the mistake. If the supervisor waits too long, the employee may forget circumstances that contributed to the way he did the work. In the meantime, he may have legitimately believed that his work was satisfactory and may feel let down when the supervisor finally takes action. Again, employee self-esteem may suffer.

In the last chapter we discussed communication. Good communication is important in the daily appraisal process. The way you communicate with an employee, the way you bring errors to her attention, the way you deal with her compared with the way you deal with other employees indicate (to her) the way you evaluate her work—and her worth.

Even today some supervisors believe that workers shouldn't be praised for doing a good job on work they are paid to do. But these are often the same supervisors who withhold appraisal except for the occasional error or lapse in performance, then "lower the boom," frequently attacking the person instead of trying to correct a problem.

"Sally, how long have you been doing this job? Look at this. Don't you know how to do the job by now? I've told you a million times that the yellow copy goes in front of the blue copy. Just because I said I wanted that order in five minutes, I didn't mean that I wanted it wrong. All these other people know how to do it right." He looked at the other workers, "Don't you?"

In this case, Sally may have been doing the job for years with the yellow and the blue copies in their proper places, and the error may have been so insignificant that it wasn't worthy of being called to Sally's attention. Sam has chosen to accentuate a single lapse on a rush project rather than recognize Sally's usually exemplary performance. Will Sally's self-esteem be damaged by Sam's outburst—or will she just see it as further verification that Sam is an insensitive, unreasonable supervisor?

How could Sam have better handled the situation? He could have realized that he had caused Sally to rush through the work and understood that Sally's simple mistake was a minor one and not mentioned it at all. If there could have been a problem from the forms being reversed, he could have mentioned it and shown Sally without attacking her and her ability to do the job. He could have merely asked her to reassemble the papers while showing her that the two sheets were out of order. This would have made her aware of the error in a way that would cause her to remember and to be more careful when rushed.

Of equal importance is where he chose to admonish Sally. Look at the last thing Sam said to Sally. "All these other people know how to do it right, don't you?" Obviously, Sam admonished Sally in the presence of other employees. This leads to Richardson's third law of performance appraisal.

RICHARDSON'S THIRD LAW OF PERFORMANCE APPRAISAL:
Praise in public, censure in private.

If you have something good to say about an employee's work, it gives that person a definite self-esteem boost if you say it so that other workers can hear. But you must be consistent in dealing with all workers in the same way. If you praise one for his day-to-day work, do the same for the others whose work calls for recognition. This, of course, does not apply to the periodic formal performance appraisal that should be done in private.

On the other hand, if an employee's performance is less than satisfactory or if he makes an error—other than a minor lapse that can be brought to the worker's attention in a quiet, non-threatening way—deal with the problem in private. This does two things. It preserves the worker's self-esteem by not embarrassing the employee in the presence of his co-workers, and it gives the worker an opportunity to explain in private the reason for the performance. He may have been following instructions as he interpreted them, or he may have been unsure of how to do a certain part of the work and was uncomfortable in asking for help. Of course it may have resulted from poor judgment.

Another example of poor supervisory technique comes to mind. (Over the years, I have observed—and in some cases been the victim of—many examples of less than satisfactory ways supervisors have dealt with their employees.)

Sam dashed into the office and gave Sally a rush job that called for digging out some remote data, converting it to usable statistical format, and having it ready for presentation to Sam's higher-ups in a matter of minutes. As soon as he completed his hurried instructions, he was out the door—with a slam—without giving Sally an opportunity to give feedback or to ask questions.

A couple of Sally's co-workers pitched in to help her,

well aware that Sally could not meet Sam's deadline without assistance. As they worked, questions were asked with most being answered with shrugs or I-don't-knows. As Sally was finishing, Sam again rushed into the office, grabbed the sheets Sally had prepared, and slammed the door again on his way out. Sally was left standing at her desk, mouth open, trying to ask a question or make an explanation. She sat down with a look of resignation on her face.

Twenty minutes later most of those in the office jumped—startled by Sam's throwing the door open. Red-faced and jaw set, Sam stomped into the twelve-person "bullpen," pointed at Sally, and shouted, "Sally, you let me down!" He wadded the papers she had prepared and threw them in her general direction. "Get in my office!"

Everyone could hear the tongue lashing that Sally endured for the next ten minutes. The entire group worked silently for some time after Sally came back to her desk, her eyes filled, and her chin quivering.

Those of us who were not already looking for another job began doing so the next day.

What the supervisor did not realize—possibly would not have cared anyway—was that his words constituted a form of performance appraisal. He gave Sally a poor rating, and he admonished her in the presence of others. The root of his problem with Sally was, of course, poor communication on his part. He did not communicate his instructions clearly, and neither asked for nor permitted feedback.

Before we go into a discussion on periodic, formal performance appraisals, it is necessary that I stress the importance of day-to-day appraisal in businesses that do or do not have a periodic appraisal system. If your business does not have one, it is vitally important that your daily contact with your workers gives them an accurate picture of your feelings about their work.

THE FORMAL PERFORMANCE APPRAISAL.

The formal appraisal should provide the supervisor the opportunity to accomplish five things:
1. Accurately evaluate the work of each employee based on a prescribed set of standards.
2. Identify training needs.
3. Identify employees with potential for advancement.
4. Identify employees whose work is marginal or unacceptable, and provide legal documentation for demotions, reassignments, or dismissal.
8. Make an overall analysis of workers' performance in a way that provides for introspection of your performance as supervisor.

The first four of these reasons, I believe, need no explanation. The fifth, however, is a reason for a periodic, formal appraisal process that too few supervisors recognize.

The formal appraisal should give the supervisor an opportunity to spread out the appraisal sheets and take a good hard look at how she has rated her workers. She should look at each individual appraisal, but more important, she should analyze them overall to find out if there are identified areas of weakness that are fairly consistent throughout the employee ratings.

If she finds that a significant number of workers are rated low in a certain area, she should first look at the training the workers have had. If the training has not been adequate, she should give or request more and better training and consider giving higher ratings pending additional training.

Second, she should look at the tools the workers are provided to do the work. Is supervision/management expecting space-age products but providing the workers horse-and-buggy era tools? Should the work be computerized? Are the workers at least given calculators if they have to do mathematic computations? Are procedures up to date? Is paperwork burdensome? Is the work being done at the right place in the organization, or is it out of character with the rest of the work done by the group? Are the workers qualified to do the work? How about workflow? If the work involves more than one person, does the work flow without interruption or bottlenecks?

Next, she should look at the work facilities. Is the space adequate? How about lighting? Ventilation? Air conditioning? Heat? Noise level?

Last, and most important, she should examine her own attitude toward the work. If she doesn't like it, feels that it is unimportant, or below the level of work normally assigned the group, she may find that her ratings are reflections of her own attitudes. It is quite a task for a supervisor to inspire others to do work she finds unimportant. And it is even more difficult for employees to turn out exemplary work when they know their supervisor considers it unimportant.

So, we find that one of the most important parts of the formal appraisal process can be the opportunity it affords the supervisor to take a look at the group in terms of employee training, tools and facilities, the work assigned the group, and her own performance as a supervisor.

Many employees feel that the periodic formal performance appraisal serves only one purpose: to give the supervisor an opportunity to perform administrative C.P.R. on any mistakes an employee made over the rating period, ponder over them for a while, inflate them completely out of proportion, and then lower the boom. Often, this attitude is justified because the supervisor may record every error and ignore good performance.

"Why, hell, that's what we pay them for!" Of course that's what you pay them for—to do the job they're paid to do, and to do it well. So if they are doing the job well, tell them so. Don't be like the supervisor who called his employees into his office one at a time. He sat slumped, elbow on desk, chin in hand, and made the following appraisal: "I don't guess you've done anything really wrong." He pushed the obligatory form across the desk. "Sign this." Every employee was rated down the middle. Nobody's performance was bad ...but nobody's was good. Everybody got a "C" on everything. Total elapsed time: 20 seconds each—probably a record for doing a poor job of performance appraisal.

WHAT'S WRONG WITH MOST APPRAISAL SYSTEMS?

1. Annual performance appraisals are too far removed from the work being appraised. Because of this, appraisals are frequently based on most recent performance or on some particular errors, or a single instance of superior work that the supervisor can remember.

2. They take time. Some supervisors believe that time spent on employees is not productive time even though if properly performed, a good performance appraisal can be some of the most productive time a supervisor can spend.

3. Supervisors are not trained to make effective appraisals.

4. Some systems are based on traits such as neatness, or politeness, and being a team player rather than the worker's performance. The supervisor's rating may be based on such things as sex, race, age, type of position the worker is filling.

The supervisor may have little direct contact with the employee being rated. He sits in his office ninety-percent of the time and knows almost nothing about the work or the workers. I know of a high level manager who decided to visit the office of a division chief who reported directly to him. Twenty minutes later he happened on the right office—the one the division chief had occupied for nearly a year—just a few feet down the hall. The only time he saw his subordinates was at meetings in his own office.

Most systems and their users do not consider the fact that even the poor performer should come away from the rating interview with his self-esteem intact.

````
````

HOW DO WE IMPROVE OUR APPRAISAL SYSTEMS?

1. Train everyone at all levels in the proper methods of using the system, and make it apply to all levels of the organization.
2. Base the system on the individual's job description, predetermined performance standards, and goals established as a joint effort by the employee and the supervisor.
3. Use several sources that may include co-workers, customers, other supervisors, and even the employee himself. You might be surprised to find that an employee is more critical of his own performance than you are, and may even be quicker than you in identifying areas where additional training is needed.
4. Design the system so that it takes into account past, present, and future performance by looking at past goals and establishing goals for the future.
5. Use the system to identify coaching and mentoring needs of the worker, and to identify formal training needs.
6. Use periodic, informal updates. A brief review of goals and accomplishments every few weeks will reinforce the validity of established goals and the importance of reaching them.
7. Give each employee a copy of the rating sheet used for the appraisal, ask him to evaluate himself, and to bring it to the appraisal interview.
8. SIMPLIFY, SIMPLIFY, SIMPLIFY. A system that is too complex or time consuming is self-defeating because supervisors will eventually short cut or ignore it.

THE APPRAISAL INTERVIEW

No system can be meaningful unless the face-to-face interview between the employee and supervisor is conducted in a manner that is worthwhile to both participants. It should be held in private, and be conducive to two-way, give-and-take communication. The supervisor should never approach the interview in a way that says to the worker, "I'll do the talking. No questions, no excuses. You will accept my evaluation of your work with neither discussion nor recourse."

Use the appraisal form completed by the employee as the base point for the interview. Look at his ratings and discuss them before showing the employee the form you have completed. You should be prepared to provide details on any part of the work that you have rated lower than the worker's own appraisal. By the same token, be prepared and willing to make changes to your evaluation when justified as the result of the comparison of the ratings.

By using the employee's own rating as a starting point, you have told the employee that you trust him to look at both his strengths and weaknesses, and that you are willing to consider changes to your ratings. This can be a powerful self-esteem enhancer because it gives him a sense of control over his destiny with the organization.

THE GOOD, THE BAD, AND THE UGLY TASK

It is easy to evaluate the work of the exceptional employee. It is a pleasant task, and few employees ever question the rating, but supervisors find that the most difficult and unpleasant part of performance appraisal is telling a worker that his performance is marginal or unsatisfactory. No one likes to be the bearer of bad tidings, but this is one of your responsibilities as supervisor. If you can't confront the poor performers, and you let them feel that their performance is acceptable, you may find the effectiveness of your unit declining. The consequence may be a poorer than expected rating when your own supervisor calls you into her office for your appraisal interview.

So how do you approach poor performance? The worker's self-appraisal may provide entry into the unpleasant task. They usually know when some of their work is not up to par with that of the others, and most of them will be honest in their evaluation. For the worker who rates his performance better than you do, his rating does provide you with a starting point. But again, be prepared to back up your ratings with specifics.

There is an approach to rating poor performance that is sometimes called the BALONEY SANDWICH method. While I do not approve of that descriptive name because it conjures a note of insincerity, it will help you appraise the employee's work without crushing her self-esteem. This method calls for an approach of ...Good performance / poor performance / good performance. In other words, the poor rating is sandwiched between two good ones.

"Sally, your work on the AAA accounts has been good. I agree with your own rating on that part of your work. You have handled those very well." (Discussion)

"On item two, I haven't rated you as high on your work on the BBB accounts. Let's talk about this." (Followed by explanation of your rating—with open-minded discussion exploring such things as your explanations about the work, coaching, or training needs. LISTEN TO THE WORKER; she may understand her needs better than you do.)

"All right, now that we have agreed on how we can improve your performance on the BBB accounts, let's go on to the CCC accounts. This is one of your best areas. Those accounts are difficult to handle." (Discussion ...be specific in discussing both high and lower ratings.)

What has Sam accomplished with this approach? He started off with a positive. He didn't shoot Sally down as soon as she walked through the door. Next, he gave specifics as to why he considered her performance on the BBB accounts lower---but with an open mind that permitted discussion, and gave Sally an opportunity to defend herself. Sam finished on another positive note that left Sally feeling good about her work, and an understanding that she and Sam would work together on improving her performance on the BBB accounts.

Sally's self-esteem remained intact, or suffered little damage.

THE UNSALVABLE EMPLOYEE

In the last part we dealt with the salvable employees; the ones who can be made fully productive workers with a certain amount of help. But how do we approach the worker who has been given every opportunity to improve his work but has not done so? How do we tell him that he will no longer be employed by the organization? Most important, how can we do it with the least negative effect on his self-esteem?

Start by asking the employee to appraise his own performance. Ask him to judge how well he has met the goals and standards that were established for his position. If his evaluation agrees with yours, your job is simplified. If he believes that his work has been satisfactory, your job is more difficult. This is when you use the documentation referred to earlier in this chapter as one of the reasons for having an appraisal system. If you have done your job properly, you have, several times, discussed his performance with him, pointed out his problem areas and offered help in training, coaching, and mentoring. The dates and the resulting agreements should have been documented when they took place. Show him his production compared with the standards established for his job. If your case for dismissal has been properly documented, he should have no recourse.

Again, this is the time to use the baloney sandwich. Start by recognizing a positive aspect of his employment. This can be as seemingly innocuous as the fact that he was punctual, or polite with customers; but find something positive. Close with another positive. This may be recognition of some talent or skill he demonstrated that would be valuable in another job.

"Sam, I asked you to use one of our appraisal forms to evaluate your own performance. Let's start by taking a look at your sheet . (Review Sam's sheet)... Now let's look at my evaluation. We agree that you have not met the production goals on the AAA accounts: the goals that we set together two months ago. But we don't agree on how well you have done on the BBB and the CCC accounts. Let's look at the goals and the production records. As you can see, you are more than ten percent below standards and more than fifteen percent below the lowest performance in the group." (NOTE: when comparing performance in this manner do not show names of other employees.)

"Sam, you try hard and you are always willing to work overtime. You always abide by the rules; you are always on time. As far as your efforts are concerned, I can only say that you are a good employee."

"But, as you can see from the production figures, you have not been able to meet company standards. You have been given remedial training, and you agreed to reach standards by this week. I now have to do one of those tasks that are difficult for a supervisor ...especially when the employee has tried so hard. As you have probably guessed, I have to give you this written notice of your termination effective this Friday."

"Sam, I believe you will agree that this is not the best type of work for you. Your grades from the community college and our discussions during the lunch period indicate that you have a real interest and talent in electronics. I hope that you can find something in that field. I believe that you can certainly excel in that type of work. Whatever you do, I want to wish you good luck."

Yes, this takes more time than walking into the work area, handing Sam a pink slip, and announcing in a voice the others can hear, "I've warned you that you had to start producing, but you aren't worth a d--- at this work. We need people who want to work. Get your stuff and get out." But the extra time is time well spent. You have shown respect for Sam as a person, recognized his uniqueness, and allowed him to leave with his self-esteem virtually intact—damaged to some degree, yes, but not crushed.

There has also been another benefit of your action: Sam will probably leave with good feelings toward you and the company. He certainly can't "bad mouth" you for being crude and non-caring. Besides, someday your business might need electronic equipment, and Sam might be the president of the only company that can supply it.

HONESTY

Be honest in your appraisals. Your employees will know—and your superiors will eventually come to know—if you are dishonest in your performance appraisals. The workers will know if you rate Sally high because she's cute and flirts with you, but does mediocre work. They will also know if you rate Sam down because he wears bow ties—which you can't stand—or because of his ethnicity, age, or because he happens to be a threat to you because he is highly intelligent. (The same could apply, of course, to female employees.)

Don't rate the borderline or poor performer's work as satisfactory because of your own insecurities that won't let you do anything that might result in a confrontation. Honesty (with statistical evidence to back you up) will survive the confrontation.

Now we have reached the point where we have to look at how a good performance appraisal system—formal or informal, day-to-day, or periodic—can improve, or help maintain the self-esteem of your work force by providing the four conditions that must be met for high self-esteem.

SENSE OF CONNECTIVENESS

There should be no question that a worker would feel a sense of connection with the organization when the ratings of his performance—day-to-day or periodic—tell him that his performance is good. But how can a worker have this feeling when some of his work is rated borderline or unacceptable?

If the supervisor stresses the good performance and encourages the worker to improve, gives needed coaching or training, and involves him in establishing goals toward improving his work, the worker can still feel a connection to the organization. This sense of connectiveness disappears quickly when the employee is chastised for his errors or threatened with dismissal.

SENSE OF POWER OR CONTROL

No matter whether an employee's work is rated high or low, she can still have a sense of power or control over her destiny, provided that she can be assured that good performance can be rewarded by advancement or by higher pay. If the worker who is rated low in some aspects of her work understands that improved performance can positively affect her future, if she is encouraged to improve, and she believes that she can improve, she can still have a sense of power or control over her future.

SENSE OF UNIQUENESS

An effective performance appraisal should not be limited to a review of hard and fast performance standards and goals, but should go beyond those to recognize any special work that has been done outside that normally expected. This may be work usually done by another person or projects outside the scope of the worker's responsibility. As an example, an employee with drawing or writing skills might be called on to help another department prepare a manual, or even announcements for the company picnic. Another example might be the clerical employee who has a special gift for making minor repairs to office equipment.

By recognizing good performance unique to the individual in both normal work assignment and the "above and beyond," we let him know that we recognize his uniqueness and his versatility.

When we recognize the uniqueness of our workers, the organization also benefits by identifying in-house skills that might be used full time should such a need occur. By doing this, management may obviate the need for recruiting from the outside and reassign or promote a worker on board. By reassigning or promoting internally, management tells its employees that it recognizes the uniqueness, skills, and talents of those in the organization.

A SENSE OF ROLE MODELS

By establishing a meaningful performance appraisal system, formal or informal, and using it effectively, management shows the worker that it expects everyone in the organization to observe rules and carry out the programs established within the organization. The supervisor who does a half-hearted job at evaluating and appraising worker performance gives the signal to the workers that not only is the work unimportant, but the performance appraisal system established by management is unimportant and insignificant.

The supervisor sends the clear message, "Don't bother to perform well; it doesn't mean anything. I don't respect the organization or its programs, so you don't need to either." The supervisor who makes good use of the system lets his workers know that they are valuable and respected, and that the appraisal system is valuable and respected.

In this chapter there was discussion on the use of goals in the performance evaluation process. In the next chapter we will look further into goals, how they should be structured, who should participate in their establishment, and how they can improve performance

Chapter 11

GIVE ME A TARGET

In the early years of this century Fredrick W. Taylor, who is known as the founder of scientific management, developed the task concept as a way of motivating blue-collar employees. His idea called for managers to assign specific tasks, quotas, performance deadlines, production objectives, and time lines. Some fifty years later management expert Peter Drucker coined the title "Management by Objectives" which involved managers in the establishment of objectives—or goals—for all parts of the organization and for all types of work.

It soon became evident that goal setting worked as a way to increase production. But goal-setting had been the job of the manager. The job of the worker was to meet those goals—to hit the targets provided by people over them. People who were not directly involved in doing the work required the workers who did to meet those goals.

The next logical step was to conduct studies to determine whether or not worker involvement in the goal-setting process would have additional positive results. A number of studies were carried out with the results being generally similar. One group of workers was assigned goals established by management; the other group took part in setting their own goals. While the production of both groups increased, the group that took part in setting their own goals generally set higher goals for themselves than the managers set for the other group. In such studies as those conducted by Edwin A. Locke in 1968, it was found that hard or difficult goals resulted in better performance than did easy goals or the "do your best" general goal. Locke noted, however, that the key to high performance when difficult goals are established is acceptance of those goals by the people required to meet those goals. If goals are too difficult, there is a greater possibility of rejection on the part of the workers.

While research did not clearly indicate a higher level of performance in the case of participative goals vs. assigned goals, there is a definite benefit derived from participative goal setting: the positive effect on the worker's self-esteem.

Before we venture into the discussion of benefits to the individual participant's self-esteem, let's look at goals and what they involve.

RICHARDSON'S FIRST LAW OF GOAL-SETTING:
Goals should be specific and positive.

To be meaningful, goals must be specific. A goal to increase sales is not specific. This does not tell you or your workers what to work for. Is one percent enough of an increase—if it is reached in three, or four, or five years? If you give a person a rifle and tell him to shoot, he will probably ask, "At what?" If you tack a bull's-eye target to a stake and tell him to hit the center of the bull's-eye, he has a specific target. He knows where he should shoot and what you want him to hit.

So it should be with goals for your workers and for yourself. A goal to increase sales by ten percent by December 31st is a specific goal. It gives both the desired increase and the date for its accomplishment.

Negative goals are self-defeating. If you have a goal to run your competition out of business, your attitude can spill over in other parts of your life and become a liability. Positive goals aimed toward improving your product or service, or public image are all positive goals that result in positive attitudes. Positive attitudes, in turn, result in a better work atmosphere where both workers and customers are more comfortable.

RICHARDSON'S SECOND LAW OF GOAL-SETTING
Goals must have a payoff.

If you set a goal for an employee, he is not likely to expend the extra effort that may be required to reach that goal unless there is some positive payoff for that employee. Can you imagine a supervisor who would tell his workers that they have to increase both the quality and quantity of their production (a goal set by the supervisor) so that "...I'll get a big raise." In some cases, of course, the workers might be delighted to work harder if it meant that the boss would be moved to another part of the organization.

Make certain that there is something in it for the people who are given the job of reaching the goal ...of hitting the bull's eye. The prize may be higher wages, one-time monetary award, a plaque, some other type award, or—if competition with another group is involved—the mere satisfaction of winning. But such competition is only effective for work over a relatively short, single period of time. Otherwise, the goal becomes merely an increase in work without an increase in compensation.

RICHARDSON'S THIRD LAW OF GOAL-SETTING
Goals must be realistic and reasonably attainable.

A goal that is unrealistic and not attainable is not a goal ...it is a wish or a dream... or plain unrealistic thinking. It must take into account the possibility of the unplanned interfering with the work and a margin for error.

"Our production for the past four years has been one thousand units a month, ten percent error rate with twenty percent overtime, but as CEO of this corporation I hereby establish the following goals: reduce the number of employees by one half, eliminate overtime, turn out two thousand error-free units a month, and insist on higher employee morale and loyalty." (That should get me a bonus of a couple of million dollars.) Realistic and reasonably attainable? Absolutely not, even though this type thinking seems to have become pretty normal over the past few years couched in such terms as "build down," "down sizing," "streamlining," and the ever-popular "belt-tightening." (Whose belt???)

When an unrealistic goal is established for an organization, the employees will recognize that it is not reasonable and will respond by either chuckling to themselves and going about their work in their normal way, by responding with minimal change, or—if the goal is completely unreasonable—rebelling. You cannot ask a worker to reach for an unreachable goal.

RICHARDSON'S FOURTH LAW OF GOAL-SETTING
The results of reaching the goal must be observable.

The mission of our unit is to build fribbles. Fribbles are the left-hand threaded pieces that attach to gribs to make a single, oscillating zornk. (The pride and joy of our company). The problem is that no one keeps records to show just how many fribbles we build every week. No tallies, no charts, no production figures. The fribbles we finish are carted out of the area on an unscheduled basis and stored somewhere until somebody wants some of them to attach to gribs. Now, the boss says we have to build twenty percent more. We don't know how many we will have to build because we don't know how many we built in the past.

The point is that, to be meaningful, goals must have measurable results. Even better, the results should be observable by not only those who work to reach those goals, but by others—management or others not in the immediate work group—as well. How will the workers know they have made twenty percent more fribbles unless there are charts, graphs, or tallies of some sort that show how much more effort is needed to reach their goal, or that they have reached it?

Imagine how satisfying it would be if the supervisor asked for twenty percent more warehouse space when a specific goal was set, and the employees could see the old warehouse space and the additional twenty percent fill up from day to day. It is not difficult to picture employees becoming excited and working harder as a result of their supervisor showing his confidence in their ability to reach the goal by reserving space for the twenty percent, and their enthusiasm as the additional space filled with evidence of their harder work.

RICHARDSON'S FIFTH LAW OF GOAL-SETTING
Put goals in writing.

When do New Year's resolutions become goals? When they reach the first four criteria (laws) above and when we put them in writing. When do we break those resolutions that are solid goals? When we don't write them down so that we are reminded of them from day to day.

Why does a supervisor need to put goals for his workers in writing? First, it shows that the supervisor is serious about those goals and dedicated to meeting them. Second, it serves as a reminder for all. It helps protect against the memory lapses that provide escape from our resolutions.

But don't write down your goals and then hide them away in a drawer where neither you nor your workers will see them. You are more apt to forget them if you can't see them. A year later you may pull that dusty folder from the back of your bottom desk drawer and wonder what is in it. "Oh, yeah, I remember writing that down. Oh, well, maybe next year." Put them where they can be seen, where they will remind you every day.

If your goal is important to the organization, to you, and to the employees, it is worth putting out for everyone to see. Try posters, or small desk signs for an office. An easy reminder is a 3"X5" card folded lengthwise so it will stand up, with a reminder of the group's goal printed on it. A few words can serve as a reminder.

RICHARDSON'S SIXTH LAW OF GOAL SETTING:
The goal must NOT have negative side effects.

A goal should never be set if its attainment will prevent the accomplishment of another goal or interfere with other work of the organization.

DIRECTED VS PARTICIPATIVE GOALS

DIRECTED GOALS
Directed goals are those that come to workers from somewhere higher up the organization chart. They may be reasonable and attainable, but they may as likely be set without adequate knowledge of the work involved in meeting them because the people who establish the goals are too far removed from the work place. A very real problem with directed goals is that the workers who are given the job of meeting those goals have no investment in them.

PARTICIPATIVE GOALS
Participative goals, on the other hand, are devised with the help and input from those at the lower end of the organization chart, at the level in the organization where the work is to be done. When workers have an investment in the form of involvement in the goal setting process, they feel an obligation to reach that goal. To do otherwise would mean letting themselves down. This is motivation at its best.

The benefit of participative goals is more than motivation alone. By involving everyone in the goal-setting process, the supervisor gets the benefit of the collective brains of the group. In most organizations the workers discuss among themselves easier and more productive ways of doing the work, but these ideas never reach the ears of supervisors or managers because the workers are not encouraged to contribute to the work planning process. They may be discouraged from making any suggestions. When this is the case, employees quickly develop the attitude of, "What's the use, management never listens to us," and they're probably right. Don't be one of those supervisors who believe that workers are stupid and never have any valuable ideas ...after all, most supervisors and managers come up from the ranks of the workers... didn't you?

Use the creativity of your group, but do not use that creativity only for setting goals. Use it to learn new methods of reaching those goals. The people who do the work usually have the best ideas about how to do it better.

DIFFICULT GOALS INTO EASY GOALS

As noted earlier in this chapter, workers are more apt to reject goals they view as too difficult—and acceptance of goals is the key to their accomplishment. How then can we set the difficult goal with more assurance of acceptance? The answer often is to break down the goal into steps and establish those steps as individual goals.

For many years I was a volunteer adult leader with the Boy Scouts of America: Scoutmaster, Cubmaster, board member, etc. Frequently, boys would look at the requirements for a skill award or a merit badge and would be overwhelmed by the number of things they had to do for the award or badge. Sometimes the requirements for a merit badge would cover two pages of the merit badge book. I would sit down with the overwhelmed scout, cover all but the first requirement with a sheet of paper, and ask the boy if he could do that first requirement. The answer was always, "Yes." Then, I would arrange the paper so that only the second requirement was visible, and so forth through all the tasks.

By reducing the big, threatening tasks to a series of less difficult goals, the boys generally were more willing to take on the requirements with little hesitation. They had a feeling of accomplishment as they met each goal, along with a boost of self-esteem.

While as a supervisor you will not be working with

young boys, you certainly can, in your work area, use the same idea of breaking down the big, overwhelming tasks into a series of attainable goals aimed at reaching the same objective. This technique can work well in reaching personal goals, or in working with your children.

The thought of writing a book can be overwhelming, but the goal of writing a chapter is not as daunting. A couple of weeks ago I set a goal to write a chapter about goals. When I finish this chapter, I will pat myself on the back, feel good about meeting that goal, and set a new goal to write the next chapter. Eleven times I have set a goal to write a chapter about a given subject, and, so far, I have met ten of them and believe I will reach number eleven this week. I don't think I could ever write a book, but I can certainly write chapters that meld together as a book.

GOALS IN THE PLANNING PROCESS

The boss says we have to have to develop plans for next year, then long-range plans for the next three years. We have to predict our needs in terms of people, training, communications, facilities, raw materials, transportation, etc. I get out my calculator, my analysis pad, and a pencil and start to work ...WAIT!! What are we going to do next year, and the year after that, and... What are our goals for next year, and the following years? Are we going to be satisfied to make the same number of fribbles we made last year?

The boss has now learned that we have to keep accurate records of our production ...so we have production records. He has also learned the importance of setting goals. He called in all the supervisors and we worked together to set realistic, attainable goals. Our goal is to increase production by ten percent next year. We also set a goal of reducing returned, defective fribbles by twenty percent. We set goals for each succeeding year. Now we know our targets. Now we have bases for building our plans for each year. We can predict our needs in terms of people, material, and money.

````
````

Next, I will get my workers together and we will set our individual and group goals. I have a feeling that they will like being included in the goal-setting/planning process of the company.

Only by setting goals can we plan for the future with any degree of accuracy.

We find, then, that goals provide targets for your workers. They know what is expected of them. Goals, therefore, help motivate those workers. But what has this to do with self-esteem? I have purposely avoided any direct reference to how goal setting (particularly participative goal-setting) can affect the self-esteem of your workers. By now you have learned how your actions can enhance self-esteem by helping provide the four conditions that must exist for a person to have high self-esteem. I will give one short sentence on how goal setting contributes to those conditions. I ask that you add your own thoughts. Find out how much you have learned—and feel good about yourself.

SENSE OF CONNECTIVENESS:

By letting employees participate we tell them that we know they are smart enough to contribute their ideas in setting goals for the group.

SENSE OF POWER OR CONTROL:

By participating in the setting of goals they will be asked to

meet, employees realize that they have a part in determining their work situation and their future.

SENSE OF UNIQUENESS:
 "Those were my ideas and mine alone. Now they have been incorporated into the goals for the group.

SENSE OF ROLE MODELS:
 By demonstrating that you are open to their thoughts and ideas, you have shown the work environment you want for the group.

 You, the supervisor, are loaded with work. You have several employees who have demonstrated that they are capable of performing at a higher level, and that they can take on some additional work. But there is no way you can offer a promotion. There is a way to distribute some of your work among your workers without abdicating your role as the leader while at the same time enhancing the employees' self esteem.

In the next chapter we will explore delegation

Chapter 12

YOU WANT ME TO DO THAT?

A few years ago Jim Jones started a part-time business in his garage. He manufactured a unique item that was fairly easy and inexpensive to make. At first, he sold a few to friends. Soon, other people who saw them wanted them. Jim quit his job and started working full time in his garage. Soon he had to rent space to store his raw materials. Things went well and Jim hired a man to help make the items so he could spend more time selling. He made up small newspaper ads and kept his own books.

Demand increased. Jim worked days, nights, and weekends. There was too much work, so as the business grew he moved it into a larger facility, hired a secretary, a bookkeeper, two sales persons, more assemblers, and a couple of people to box and ship the items. Today he is the CEO of Jones Corporation with three plants making a hundred different products including high tech components for the space program. Jim reads production reports, watches the price of company stock (of which he holds the majority), plays golf three afternoons a week, and travels to "exotic locales "on company business."

In short, Jim learned how to delegate. He found out that he could not do all the work. He had fumbled his way through the variety of tasks when the business was not so complicated, but when the workload became too heavy and the tasks too complex for one person, he hired appropriate people and delegated authority to perform specific parts of the work to each of them.

Whenever we look at an organization chart, what we are seeing is a graphic illustration of delegation at work. The C.E.O. delegates certain authority to those reporting directly to him. Each delegates some of that authority to his subordinates.

This follows down to the lowest level of the organization.

Delegation is not a new concept. A few thousand years ago Moses' father-in-law took Moses aside and said (paraphrased), "Moses, you've got too much work for one person. Your wife is complaining that you're never home. You're killing yourself trying to judge all the cases that come to you. Find some smart guys and make them lower court judges. Let them decide the less important cases."

Moses frowned. "I don't know if I can find qualified..."

"Qualified, shmalified! Of course there are qualified people out there. Just look around. Trust me. Trust your people. Delegate, man, delegate!"

While that is one of the earliest recorded examples of delegation, there was certainly a great deal of delegation required in the building of the pyramids. Somebody had to be responsible for overall planning; somebody had to be responsible for cutting the stones, another for transporting them, another for boosting them into place. One person could not have done all those jobs.

Modern management frames delegation in the principle that work should be done at the lowest level of the organization at which the work can be done properly. Management should operate on the principle of exception. That is, management should be directly involved only in those matters that are of an exceptional nature that cannot be resolved at a lower level nor reduced to standard operating procedure. In other words, if workers earning thirty thousand dollars a year can do certain tasks properly, let them do those tasks. Don't make a supervisor or manager making twice that much do those tasks. Get the most for your dollars. Let the fifty thousand dollar employee make the fifty thousand dollar decisions.

The type of delegation discussed to this point is that involved in establishing the structure of the organization. The delegations we will discuss now are those made within divisions, branches, or sections of the organization. These are made by the mid or lower-level manager or by the supervisor. They are used to distribute work most effectively within the unit.

As an example, let's look again at our old friends Sam and Sally. Sam heads up a procurement group and Sally is one of his best workers. Sam has authority to approve purchases up to $50,000. Sally receives the requests from managers and supervisors in all parts of the organization. She reviews them for justification, compliance with rules, proper format, and to determine if the items are available at a lower price than estimated by the requestor. Sally sends the requests to Sam with her recommendation that he either approve the request or ask for additional justification.

Sam has found that Sally's recommendations are on target 99% of the time. The organization has grown during the past few years and the number of procurement actions has increased accordingly. Sam spends too much time looking over and signing requests for low cost, low priority items. Because Sally has the knowledge and the training to approve or disapprove requests, Sam decides to delegate to Sally (with the approval of higher management) authority to approve purchase requests with values up to $25,000.

Sam (the delegator) writes a memo to Sally (the delegate) with copies to anyone concerned, delegating to her authority to approve requests up to $25,000. In the memo he also gives clear limitations. In this case, Sally cannot approve requests for computer equipment. They require special review and approval. He also specifies that any conflicts or disagreements with a requestor will be referred to Sam because the requests are signed by managers at his level or higher.

Sally realizes that the delegation will make the work flow more efficiently, and, while not netting her any additional pay immediately, will give her valuable experience that could qualify her for a higher paying position--even Sam's if he should leave or be promoted. Sam, Sally, and the organization benefit from the delegation.

It is important at this point that Sam understand that delegating authority to sign requests for him only gives Sally authority to do the work and operational responsibility to do the work properly; it does not relieve Sam of the ultimate responsibility for the work. Sam has not abdicated his role; he is still in charge of the group and remains responsible for the work of the group.

Delegation can be difficult for some supervisors or managers. "If you want something done right, you have to do it yourself!" "They might make mistakes!" "I know how to do that better than anybody else!" "That's MY responsibility, and I'm not turning it over to anybody else!" This brings us to:

RICHARDSON'S FIRST LAW OF DELEGATION:
Trust.

The supervisor/manager must trust her workers to do the delegated work on time, to do it properly, to make correct decisions, and to adhere to the limitations of the delegation. If you interviewed, hired, and trained your workers, you should trust yourself to have done that job well, and trust your workers to do their work well. DELEGATION MUST BE BASED ON TRUST. You must believe that your workers can and will do the work as well as you can do it—or at least 99%-- as well as you. But trust must start before delegation. If you have demonstrated trust in your employees in the past, the delegated authority may be accepted readily. If you have not, the worker may interpret the delegation as a "sink or swim" move intended to challenge the employee's ability to do the work.

RICHARDSON'S SECOND LAW OF DELEGATION:
Be sure the delegate is ready for the work you want to delegate to her.

The delegate must have the skills, knowledge, and attitude

needed to do the work delegated to her. Before you delegate, be sure that the person understands the work and has had any training needed. While those factors are fairly easy to identify, it may be more difficult to find out if the worker's attitude is right for the work. An employee may appear to accept new duties and to smile on the outside, but may be grumbling on the inside—and possibly to other workers—that she already has too much work and shouldn't have to do the boss's work. If this attitude is detected, it may be best to work on the employee's attitude and delegate to another employee.

The delegation action should involve more than a memo. Face to face discussion is in order. The supervisor should tell the worker exactly what is delegated, the limits, the controls, any periodic review or reports that are needed. This should be the time for the employee to voice any reservations; and to ask any questions. It is also the time for the supervisor to let the worker know that being delegated authority is the result of her good work, is recognition of her value to the organization and her unique knowledge and ability. In other words, positive action by the supervisor can enhance her sense of connectiveness to the organization, sense of power or control over her future, and her sense of uniqueness.

RICHARDSON'S THIRD LAW OF DELEGATION:
Don't delegate authority to perform certain tasks because you don't like to do them—or hold on to tasks because you enjoy doing them.

Delegation is not a dumping game. It is not a way to get rid of work you find unpleasant. Delegation is a way of increasing the efficiency of the group. If the work can be done by someone working for you—and management has no objection—delegate. By the same token, don't hold on to work and refuse to delegate simply because you enjoy doing it. Consider delegation in the light of what is best for the organization—and the individual workers in your group.

````
````

RICHARDSON'S FOURTH LAW OF DELEGATION:
You cannot delegate ultimate responsibility.

Delegation does NOT mean "out of sight, out of mind." In our earlier example of Sam delegating authority to Sally to approve purchase requests, we noted that Sam still had ultimate responsibility for the work done by Sally. While Sally has authority to perform certain tasks and operational responsibility for doing the work correctly, Sam retains ultimate responsibility because he is the supervisor/manager who is accountable to management for the work of his group. He is the one management will call upon for explanation of errors, or who will receive accolades for work done well. As the supervisor of the unit, Sam is the one who should recognize good performance of the people working under him.

RICHARDSON'S FIFTH LAW OF DELEGATION:
Let go!!

If you have ever had a boss who gave you a job to do and then hovered, looked over your shoulder and told you to cross every T and dot every I, you know what it is like to have authority delegated to you while the boss keeps a string tied to the work so he could jerk it away from you at any time. If you delegate, trust and let go. Establish clear guidelines, ask for periodic reports if necessary, and let go. If you continually check up on the worker or double check the work, you are telling the worker that you don't really trust him to perform. By trusting and letting go, you can enhance the worker's self-esteem.

Avoid the subtle holding on. You haven't let go if you frequently "happen to drop by" the delegate's desk and ask, "How's it going?" "Have you checked out .....," "Did you remember....," or any such checking up that says to the delegate that you're not sure he can do the job without your close attendance.

Theodore Roosevelt said, "The best executive is the

one who has enough good sense to pick good men to do what he wants done, and self-restraint enough to keep from meddling with them while they do it." (I feel certain that today "Teddy" would have said men and women, instead of men.)

REMEMBER: DELEGATION IS A FORM OF EMPOWERMENT—IT SAYS, "I BELIEVE IN YOU."

RICHARDSON'S SIXTH LAW OF DELEGATION:
Set a standard before delegating.

This is another opportunity for you to serve as a role model. (Needed, as previously noted, for an employee to have high self-esteem.) Before you delegate work to a subordinate, be sure you have demonstrated the level of performance you expect from the employee. If you have done the work in a haphazard manner or made a lot of errors, you have little right to set a higher standard for the delegate. The delegate will have no confidence that she can come to you for assistance and get good information. Demonstrate the standard you are setting and make it clear that you expect the worker to reach that standard.

NOTE: It must be recognized that in some situations there may be employees who do highly specialized work that the supervisor is not fully qualified to perform. This is not delegated work per se, but simply the assignment of duties. The supervisor's role is to oversee and coordinate all the work of the group. An example is the secretary. Her boss may not know how to type, but her work is part of the supervisor's responsibility.

RICHARDSON'S SEVENTH LAW OF DELEGATION:
Set limits—do not over delegate.

Several times during my career I saw cases in which an employee was delegated authority that should have been retained by the manager. In other instances the employee assumed that the delegation gave him broader authority than was intended because the delegator did not clearly set forth limits of authority delegated.

In one case a staff member was delegated authority to perform a study and make recommendations for changes in work processes. The employee took a quick look and started ordering branch chiefs to make changes in procedures and in the distribution of work in their organizations. The person had neither supervisory responsibility over the branch chiefs nor the power to give such orders. He immediately became very unpopular with the branch chiefs—and his boss.

BE SURE THAT THE DELEGATE UNDERSTANDS THAT AUTHORITY DOES NOT MEAN POWER---ONLY PERMISSION.

In another case, a supervisor delegated to a subordinate authority to approve time off, give orders, reprimand, and evaluate performance of the workers in the unit. The supervisor had little skill in dealing with subordinates and preferred his working relationships to be downward only, so he abdicated his role as supervisor and became a figurehead. Sometimes, passive supervisors try to informally delegate their supervisory authority in an attempt to avoid blame for problems, or as a way to avoid confrontations with subordinates.

NEVER DELEGATE YOUR SUPERVISORY AUTHORITY TO A SUBORDINATE EXCEPT TO ACT FOR YOU TEMPORARILY IN YOUR ABSENCE.

Supervisors need vacations, too. But make sure that the person you choose to act as supervisor in your absence has the training, knowledge, skills and attitudes that will make her acceptable not only to you, but to your workers as well.

RICHARDSON'S EIGHTH LAW OF DELEGATION:
Put it in writing.

No matter if the authority delegated is fairly simple or

complex with lots of tasks involved and various limitations, it is best to put the delegation in writing. First, the delegate will know exactly what is delegated and what limitations are set. This can eliminate confusion as to what the worker can and can't do. Second, should anyone question the worker's right to act for you, she will have a formal document she can refer to or show the questioner. Third, you can refer back to the document if the delegate fails to carry out the delegated work. (In this case, use it to identify any confusion or to determine any training needed.) Fourth, you can use the document in the performance evaluation process.

I have used a simple way to avoid confusion. When I delegated authority to subordinates I used the required obfuscating language in the formal memorandum, then attached a simple check list that the delegate could use as a guide rather than plow through paragraphs to find an answer to questions of what and how much.

THREE ASPECTS OF DELEGATION:
There are three basic aspects of delegation:
1. The assignment of duties by the manager or supervisor,
2. The creation of an obligation on the part of the worker to satisfactorily perform the duties assigned.
3. The granting of permission by the delegator to make commitments, use the organization's resources, and take action necessary to perform the duties,

Only when all three aspects are present is delegation complete. Frequently managers or supervisors have no problem with aspects 1 and 2, but fail to realize that the delegate may not be able to do the job expected without concomitant authority to make commitments, use resources, and take action. The same person would never hire a secretary and tell her not to answer the telephone unless told to do so, and not provide her with a desk, word processor, paper, or pencil. It is unfair to hold a worker accountable for results if he is not permitted to use resources needed or to take action based on his own best judgment.

Throughout this chapter I have made references concerning delegation and self-esteem. Now it is time for you to give thought as to how delegation, done properly, helps contribute to the four conditions that must be available for a person to have high self-esteem. This time, you are on your own!

SENSE OF CONNECTIVENESS:

_____

SENSE OF POWER OR CONTROL:

_____

SENSE OF UNIQUENESS:

_____

SENSE OF ROLE MODELS:

_____

Leaders know the importance of delegation, both in

terms of its value to the organization and its value to the delegates. A leader cannot lead without delegating authority to his/her followers. Next, we will learn more about leadership, and help you find out if you are truly a leader.

Chapter 13
(12 B if you're superstitious)

IF YOU'RE OUR LEADER, GET OUT IN FRONT

Does your organization operate on the premise that everybody is a member of a team given the assignment of accomplishing the work of the group, or does it suffer from the US/THEM syndrome? The US/THEM syndrome appears in organizations that make such distinction between those who manage or supervise and those who do the work that there appears to be a caste system or adversarial relationship that separates management from employees, supervisors from workers. If this is the case where you work, you are a victim of the management style that has dominated in this country for the last hundred or so years.

How did the US/THEM syndrome come about? Between the years of 1880 and 1920 this country experienced tremendous growth. In those forty years the population doubled. With this growth came increased demand for goods and materials, so businesses expanded and created the type internal structure we know today: divisions, branches, sections, etc. As an example of the growth in businesses, in 1870 McCormick Reaper was one of the nation's largest manufacturers with 500 employees. Thirty years later seventy factories employed thousands of workers. Several had 6,000 to 10,000 workers. A perplexing problem came about when managers tried to hire workers to satisfy the huge increase in demand. The immigrants who were responsible for the increased demand were, in turn, the source of the labor force needed to meet that demand. But many were uneducated and unskilled; many spoke little or no English. To complicate matters, training was minimal at best, working conditions were barely tolerable, and turnover was high, so high, in fact, that the Ford Motor Co. had to hire 24,000 people in one year to maintain a work force of 13,700.

In addition, there were vastly more people available than there were jobs, so workers were considered interchangeable commodities expected to get up to production in hours or even minutes. If they couldn't produce, they were out the door to be replaced by the next person in line. The situation resulted in two assumptions on the part of management:
1. Jobs had to be reduced and defined as narrowly as possible so that almost anyone could do the work.
2. Workers required close, direct supervision.

Generally, workers were considered inept, lazy, rigid, unintelligent and unmotivated. Supervisors were considered DRIVERS who could hire, set individual pay rates (the lower, the better), hand out discipline—often in the form of physical abuse—fine workers, and fire them without explanation. It is no surprise that this was the era that saw the beginnings of labor unions in this country.

Unfortunately, some of management's attitudes have carried over to many of our present managers and supervisors. To them, management means control, setting of limitations and parameters, measurement of productivity by numbers, stability, and control through strictly enforced systems and procedures. In those cases, management has become a mechanical discipline rather than one built on people skills. Managers have become controllers instead of leaders.

Of course, some managers are leaders. However, not all managers are leaders, and not all leaders are managers.

THE DIFFERENCE BETWEEN MANAGERS AND LEADERS.

The root origin of the word MANAGE means hand. Thus, managing seems to connote handling with the focus on control ...as controlling with a strong hand.

The root origin of the word LEAD means to go. Leading connotes stepping out in front to show others the way.

So the real difference between managers and leaders is their way of dealing with workers or followers. The manager who is NOT truly a leader says, "...go and do the job exactly the way I tell you. I will do the planning, I will organize you, direct you, and evaluate what you do and how you do it."

The leader, on the other hand, says, "While I am responsible for leading the group, we are a team. I need your help in finding the best way to organize our resources, to plan our approach to the work to be done, to assure quality of the product by active participation, and to meet the goals of the group and the organization." This involvement in the total work process makes a great contribution to the self-esteem of the workers.

RICHARDSON'S FIRST LAW OF LEADERSHIP:
Leadership is a relationship between the leader and the followers appropriate to the situation.

An abundance of studies have been made in attempts to define leadership in terms of traits such as intelligence, charisma, self-assurance and integrity. Generally, the conclusions have been that there is no single group of traits that could be defined as fitting in all leadership situations.

Other studies looked into behavior of leaders to determine if there were certain ways leaders behaved that set them apart. One of those conducted at the University of Michigan resulted in the finding that leaders who were employee-oriented were associated with higher group productivity and greater job satisfaction. Leaders who were production-oriented and showed less regard for their followers tended to be associated with low group productivity and less worker satisfaction. As with the trait related studies, no list of behaviors resulted.

The assumptions behind the trait studies were that if
````
````

leadership ability was based on a specific set of personal traits, it could be assumed that leaders were born with those traits, and those who did not possess them could never be leaders. The behavioral studies, on the other hand, would have indicated that certain types of behavior could be learned, thus leadership could be a learned skill.

Through the years there have been many other studies that resulted in such things as managerial grids that measured a leader/managers style rather than give insight regarding leadership attributes. Others explored "contingencies" or situational factors that affect leadership, and autocratic vs. democratic styles. Later studies linked leader/follower relationship and the situation under which tasks were to be done.

If you are interested in pursuing leadership theories and studies, I recommend searching through management texts in a university library. In some you may find a chapter or so dealing with leadership while you may find that others avoid the subject completely.

So where does this take us? From my own reading on the subject and my personal experiences, I believe that leadership is based on situational relationships. This means that there is the right relationship between the leader and his followers for a given situation. The infantry sergeant must display an authoritarian/expert relationship in the situation that requires immediate decisive action. The advertising executive's situation calls for a more democratic/ open/communicative relationship that promotes originality and the exchange of ideas.

In most work situations there are some skills, known as people skills, that the best leaders will exhibit.

RICHARDSON'S SECOND LAW OF LEADERSHIP:
Leaders are people people.

Leaders care about their people. They have people skills. They know that the leader does not do things alone.
````
````

Their achievements are not theirs alone, but are reflections of the leaders' ability to meld their followers into productive entities. People skills are not ways to trick or manipulate people into doing what the leader wants. People skills are methods of dealing with others in ways that are beneficial to both the leader and their followers. Leaders work with others in ways that will enhance—or at the least not do harm to—the self-esteem of their followers.

SOME IMPORTANT PEOPLE SKILLS FOR THE LEADER:

1. Have empathy for others. Understand their feelings and take a personal interest in them. You cannot fake sincerity or regard for others. Both are necessary for you to deal with others effectively.
2. Contact your people at their work areas. Leaders don't cozy themselves in private office sanctuaries and contact their followers only when something goes wrong.
3. COMMUNICATE—COMMUNICATE—COMMUNICATE. Talk to people, ask them questions; be interested; encourage them to open up and tell you more. LISTEN—LISTEN—LISTEN. Give feedback. Expect feedback. If it doesn't come freely, ask for it.
4. Respect others. Don't forget to show the same respect to those close to you as you would to a stranger. For some reason we tend to show less respect to those we know best than to the new customer who walks in the door. Recently I read a short article dealing with respect. I read it twice because I couldn't believe what I read the first time. The writer stated that a person had to earn his respect, implying that being a human being was not enough in itself. A person had to do something that proved respect was deserved. I feel sorry for the writer. Even though I don't know him, I can picture him, nose up, eyebrows raised, looking

down on the underlings. He has most likely missed out on some great relationships.

5. Be approachable—open to others. Your attitude and physical presence let people know if they can come to you when they feel a need. You can do much by talking to others. Break the ice. If some people seem hesitant to approach you or talk to you, seek them out. A smile and a few words can do much to overcome reticence.

6. If you make a commitment, follow up. "I'll check on that and let you know," "I'll call you.

One study researched the question of what people look for in a leader. The results show that we want leaders who are:

HONEST, COMPETENT, FORWARD LOOKING, INSPIRING

Honesty was determined to be the most important of these characteristics. When the leader makes a commitment her followers know that she means what she says and will do what she says. They also know that if there must be changes, the leader will be honest in informing her followers of the reasons for the changes, and will even solicit input from them as to possibilities for a new direction.

BEHAVIOR IS THE ONLY WAY TO DEMONSTRATE HONESTY.

The leader shows honesty through his actions ...not just through his words.

Competent does not mean that the leader must be able to do all the jobs of his followers better than they can do them. It means that the leader is competent in the leadership skills needed to carry the people—thus the organization—in the right direction to get the work done. He can pick the right people for the work to be done, coordinate the efforts of the group, and appeal to the best effort from each of his followers.

Forward looking means that the leader must have a sense of where the group is going, its goals and how it is going to reach them. This does not mean that he is a visionary who can see or predict the future, only the ability to plan and to take alternate paths if planned paths are blocked.

The inspiring person is enthusiastic, energetic, and positive. He is a cheerleader, a coach, a mentor. The leader not only has a dream, but is able to communicate that dream and the anticipated results in a way that makes us want to be a part of that dream.

> "The boss drives his men;
> The leader coaches them.
> The boss depends on authority;
> The leader on good will.
> The boss inspires fear;
> The leader inspires enthusiasm.
> The boss says 'I'.
> The leader says 'we'.
> The boss fixes the blame for the breakdown;
> The leader fixes the breakdown.
> The boss says 'go';
> The leader says 'let's go.'"
>
> H. Gordon Selfridge, merchant

While an enthusiastic, energetic, and positive leader may not change the nature of the work, he certainly can make the work more enjoyable. Enthusiasm and excitement signal the leader's commitment to pursuing a purpose.

In short, leaders who display those four characteristics are considered credible. Credibility is built on trust, and as indicated in the preceding chapter on delegation, trust is a two way street. If the manager doesn't trust his workers, there is little likelihood that the workers will feel they can trust the leader.

Charles O'Reilly of the University of California concluded from a study that when top management is perceived as having high credibility and a strong philosophy, employees are more likely to:
> Be proud to tell others that they are part of the organization.
> Talk up the organization to friends.
> See their own values as similar to those of the organization.
> Feel a sense of ownership for the organization.

Emerson said, "Our chief want in life is someone who will make us do what we can." While he used the term "make us," he could have as easily said, let us. We want to work for and with someone who leads us in ways that allow us to use the talents, the intelligence, and the skills that are uniquely ours in work that challenges us. The old style manager satisfies few of these criteria. By limiting, controlling, and adhering to the status quo, she denies the workers the opportunities they seek, and denies the organization the full potential of those workers.

Nora Watson, an editor, said, "...most of us are looking for a calling, not a job. Most people have jobs that are too small for their spirits. Jobs are not big enough for people."

RICHARDSON'S THIRD LAW OF LEADERSHIP:
The leader welcomes the opportunity to try new things.

The leader welcomes new ideas, thrives on change that provides better ways, and knows how to motivate by recognizing accomplishment—even if the final result is not as good as anticipated. Leadership is an active—not passive role. Leaders do not wait for fate to smile upon them. They seek challenges in order to test their own abilities and the abilities of their followers.

Leaders experiment and take risks. Since risk-taking involves mistakes and failures, they learn to accept disappointment as a part of taking risks. The best leaders count them as learning experiences.

THREE TYPES OF LEADERS

1. The designated leader has leadership cast upon him as a consequence of the position he occupies in an organization. He demonstrates his leadership through his methods of dealing with his workers or followers.
2. The informal leader emerges from within a group as a result of her knowledge and her way of dealing with her co-workers who trust her to give accurate advice and guidance.
3. The situational leader is one who steps forward and takes charge in the isolated situation. He may be the Casper Milquetoast who quietly sat in the corner and did his work, yet suddenly became the hero who put out the flames when the office building caught fire. Afterward, he returned to his corner and went about his work as usual, the situation that was the catalyst that made him a short-time leader ended.

Whether leaders are selected for projects or initiate them, they always look for opportunities to do what is not being done while many managers rarely initiate a project; most of what they do is assigned.

RICHARDSON'S FOURTH LAW OF LEADERSHIP:
Sometimes, challenges seek leaders.

Assume that your community needs a place for teenagers to congregate, eat, have soft drinks, and listen to their music. This should be a spot that is safe and the activities supervised to insure that nothing is done that is illegal or socially unacceptable. The city leaders have set up a committee that meets every week or so but accomplishes little or nothing. The committee has selected someone to head up the meetings who is low key and has little imagination. After several months of head shaking there is consensus that nothing can be done.

Frank Frimbish has a teenage son and a daughter who will soon be a teenager. Frank has worked in the background on some youth programs with his church, the Boy Scouts of America, and Little League baseball. He likes and respects kids and has come to know what they like and dislike. He has become frustrated with the lack of activity on the part of the committee, so he approaches business leaders and property owners. There is more support than was evidenced by the reports of the committee. He prepares some rough notes and goes to the next meeting of the committee, waits through more head shaking on the part of the members, and finally gets up when there is talk of disbanding the committee.

Frank clears his throat and nervously begins telling the group the results of his informal survey. As he speaks his knees quit shaking and his voice becomes stronger. Before the evening is over Frank becomes the informal leader of the effort. A week later he is asked to become a member of the committee and soon after enthusiastically accepts the chairmanship. Six months later a ribbon is cut, opening the new teen center.

Frank has never emerged as a leader before, but this time the challenge has been hunting a leader. It tapped Frank on the shoulder and said, "Here's your chance. Here is the situation in which you will become a leader." Fortunately, Frank seized the opportunity, helped the community teenagers, and changed his own life by coming to the realization that he could be a leader.

RICHARDSON'S FIFTH LAW OF LEADERSHIP:
A leader must be able to communicate.

"Leadership and communication are inseparable." Claude I. Taylor, Chairman of the Board, Air Canada.

Certainly, a leader needs a clear vision of the organization and where it is going, but a vision is of little value unless it is shared in a way so as to generate enthusiasm and commitment. Communication skills are essential for the leader. He must be able to communicate upward and downward, and he MUST KNOW THE VALUE OF FEEDBACK AND LISTENING. I trust that it is not necessary for me to expound further on the subject of communication in this chapter. If you wish, you can turn back to the chapter on communication and breeze through it again.

RICHARDSON'S SIXTH LAW OF LEADERSHIP:
Leaders look for ways to break out of the routine.

Boring, routine tasks promote neither leadership nor high performance. Of course routine is essential in some types of work. If it were not for routine, tasks might not be done the same way each time, or with the same frequency. I prefer to fly airlines that are committed to routine in maintenance and inspections. I also prefer to drive cars that were manufactured under a system of routine inspections. The issue with leaders is not <u>routines or no routines</u>, but <u>what routines</u>. Routines that serve the organization and the customers should be preserved. Routines that do not should be identified and tossed out. Throw out routines that smother creativity.

WHY AREN'T THERE MORE LEADERS???

There are many people who are intelligent, talented, and skilled. So why do so few emerge as leaders when there are so many who could climb to the top?

First, it is easier to follow than to lead. Management does things this way, so why rock the boat? Those managers at the top got where they are by treating their jobs and their people in certain ways. It worked for them; it should work for me. Besides, it takes a lot of effort to change, and I'm getting by the way I am. Do those rationalizations sound familiar?

````
````

You may not hear them from others or say them out loud yourself, but if they sound familiar, examine your own attitudes and find out if you are guilty of being satisfied to let others lead when you could accomplish more by becoming a leader.

Second, the black curtain of fear blocks the way. Most of us are afraid of making an error and being branded a failure by others. People fear what could happen instead of what they might gain. Some fear success and the responsibility that goes along with it. They are afraid that they would not be able to meet that responsibility. This brings to the third reason.

Low self-esteem is the third reason people do not extend themselves and become leaders. If a person does not have positive feelings about himself, he is not likely to feel that he can inspire others, and cannot picture himself in the role of the leader who steps out in front and says, "follow me."

If the thought of risking, initiating, and taking that first step forward is somewhat frightening, do something about it!

It has been said that as you think, so will you act. In other words, if you think you can do something or act a certain way, you can do it. If you take that first step, that first risk, your mind will say, "That wasn't so difficult, was it? Everything came out ok. Let's do it again, or try something else—something more difficult." Each attempt will be easier than the last.

INITIATE ...TAKE THAT RISK ...TRY SOMETHING NEW ...DO IT!

Take a good hard look at yourself. Are you willing to risk? Are you willing to be the first to try something? Can you speak up and say, "I have a better way?" If so, go for it! If not, try it. Even if things don't turn out exactly as you had hoped, you can still say, "I tried, and I'll try again." You will feel better about yourself just for trying and your self-esteem will benefit.

How does good leadership enhance the self-esteem of your followers? Let's look at the four conditions needed for high self-esteem.

SENSE OF CONNECTIVENESS:

The leader treats his workers (followers) as a team with everyone sharing the responsibility for completing the work and sharing in the benefits derived from the work of the team. He lets each worker know that she is a part of the team effort. (Add your thoughts)

A SENSE OF POWER OR CONTROL:

The leader recognizes and rewards the efforts of his followers. He listens to his followers and considers their contributions and idea for improving the product or service provided by the group. As a result, the followers know that they have a degree of control over the direction of the group and their own future with the group. (Add your thoughts).

A SENSE OF UNIQUENESS:

The leader strives to know his followers and allows each of them to use the talents, skills and knowledge unique to that person to the fullest extent possible in reaching the goals of the organization. (Add your thoughts).

A SENSE OF ROLE MODELS:

The leader serves as a role model for the group. The attitudes, dedication, and demeanor of the leader serve as models for her followers. The followers look up to the true leader and model their behavior accordingly. A wise man by the name of Wain said, "Nothing motivates a man more than to see his boss putting in an honest day's work." (ADD your thoughts)

The above quotation leads us into the next chapter on motivation.

Chapter 14

WHAT IS THIS THING CALLED MOTIVATION??

Your boss shakes his finger at the group of supervisors assembled for one of his staff meetings, "All of you have to do better," he shouts, his face flushed, sweat running down his cheeks. "Productivity has to improve and errors have to go down. The brass says no more overtime, so your people have to work harder. If they can't do it, tell them we'll get people who can." He lowers his voice and stabs the air toward each of you. "And if you can't do it, I'll get somebody who can. Now get out there and motivate those dummies."

As you walk back to your work area you ponder the words of the boss. "Motivate those dummies," he had said. The word "dummies" bothers you. They are good people, and they work hard. You've told them what they have to do, and you've told them everything you think they need to know. "Motivate those dummies." Motivate. Everybody talks about motivation, but nobody ever tells you how to motivate people. What is this thing called motivation all about, and how do you learn to motivate?

That's what this chapter is about ...motivation.

The American Heritage Dictionary defines motivate: To stimulate to action; provide with an incentive or motive; impel, incite. It defines motive: an emotion, desire, psychological need, or similar impulse acting as an incitement to action. Webster's New World Dictionary defines motivate: to provide with, or affect as, a motive or motives; incite. It defines motive: some inner drive, impulse, etc. that causes one to act in a certain way; incentive; goal.

Note that the definitions of motive refer to it as an emotion, desire, psychological need, impulse, inner drive: all conditions internal to the individual. This leads to:

RICHARDSON'S FIRST LAW OF MOTIVATION:
The supervisor does not motivate; he can only create an atmosphere in which people are motivated.

That isn't the longest law in this book, but is one of the most important. As seen above, the motive for a person to act comes from within as a drive or an emotion. So it is the supervisor's or manager's job to create an atmosphere in the work place that tends to contribute to the workers' inner drives to act.

Numerous studies have been done in attempts to determine how we are motivated and what factors are involved in motivation. This in an attempt to reduce motivation to its basics and to provide a set of rigid steps or actions that a manager could follow which would assure that employees would be constantly and consistently motivated to carry out whatever tasks management would assign them. Unfortunately—or perhaps I should say fortunately—people are individuals who do not react consistently to hard and fast rules.

Several theories were developed during the 60's.

MASLOW'S HIERARCHY OF NEED THEORY:

Abraham Maslow formulated the theory of a hierarchy of needs that govern our motives.

> 1. PHYSIOLOGICAL needs: hunger, thirst, shelter, sex, and other physical needs. As those needs are satisfied...
> 2. SAFETY needs—become dominant. As safety needs of security, and protection from physical and emotional needs are substantially met, the next tier of needs become our primary motivators.
> 3. LOVE needs: affection, belongingness, acceptance, friendship.
> 4. ESTEEM needs come into play: self-respect,

autonomy, achievement, status, recognition, attention.

At the top of the pyramid are five SELF-ACTUALIZATION needs: The need to become what we are capable of becoming, including growth, achieving our potential, and self-fulfillment. Unfortunately, while there appears to be some merit to this theory, a number of studies undertaken to validate it found no scientific support.

ALDERFER

Later, Clayton Alderfer suggested that there were only three levels of needs involved in the process of motivation:
1. EXISTENCE NEEDS: Needs required for human existence. (Maslow's physiological and safety needs)
2. RELATEDNESS NEEDS: How people relate to their social environment including needs for meaningful social and interpersonal relationships.
3. GROWTH NEEDS: Alderfer's highest need category, this includes the needs for self-esteem and self-actualization.

MCGREGOR'S X-Y THEORY

Douglas McGregor founded the X-Y theory that indicates that there are primarily two views of people by administrators. Under the X theory, there are four negative assumptions held by administrators:
1. Employees inherently dislike work and try to avoid it.
2. Because they dislike work, they must be controlled, coerced, or threatened with punishment to meet goals.
3. Workers will shirk responsibilities and seek direction.
4. Workers will place security above other work factors, and will display little ambition.

Under the Y theory, McGregor cited four positive views of workers:
1. Workers can see work to be as natural as rest or play.
2. Workers will exercise self-direction and self-control if committed to the objectives of the group.
3. The average person can learn to accept, even seek

responsibility.

4. Both creativity, and the ability to make good decisions are widely dispersed and not limited to those in higher-level positions.

McGregor's work did more to examine the attitudes of supervisors and managers toward employees than to develop any insight into what motivates workers.

McCLELLAN

David McClellan proposed that there are three needs or motives in the workplace:

1. The need for achievement—to excel, the need to achieve relative to a set of standards, to strive to succeed.
2. The need for affiliation—to enjoy friendly, close interpersonal relationships.
3. The need for power—to be able to make others behave in a way they would not have done otherwise.

McClelland found that some people have a compelling drive to achieve for the sake of success alone. These higher achievers, he found, are those who look for challenges, are competitive, like to keep score, and avoid very easy or very difficult tasks.

HERZBERG

In the 60s Fredrick Herzberg made a study to determine what people wanted from their jobs. Surprising to many managers was the finding that salary did not rate as the top factor that led to extreme satisfaction on the job. The top eight of sixteen factors/motivators that led to extreme satisfaction ranked as follows:
1. Achievement
2. Recognition
3. The work itself
4. Responsibility
5. Advancement

6. Growth
7. Salary
8. Relationship with supervisor

The top eight factors/DEmotivators that resulted in extreme DISsatisfaction were ranked:
1. Company policy and administration
2. Supervision
3. The work itself
4. Achievement
5. Relationship with supervisor
6. Working conditions
7. Recognition (lack thereof)
8. Salary

This study clearly showed that money is not usually a primary motivator (unless a person does not have any). While a raise of a few hundred dollars a year may well serve as a motivator and be considered a verification of being valued as an employee to a person in the lower salary ranges, the same raise for someone at a higher income may be a viewed as an insult and verification of the employee's feelings that she is considered of little value to the organization. While there were detractors who questioned the validity of Herzberg's study (as with any study), the results did provide information that should be seriously considered by managers and supervisors when attempting to determine what factors contribute to or detract from employee motivation.

EXPECTANCY THEORY

More recently, the expectancy theory has come to the forefront. This theory asserts that the strength of the tendency to do a given thing depends on the strength of the person's expectancy that the doing will be followed by a given outcome and by how attractive that outcome will be to the person. This would infer that workers consciously calculate the payoff before taking on any task. This seems to be a rather cold and sterile theory that does not consider that people are often motivated to take action when there is little or no personal gain expected. This theory also assumes that what the organization has to offer agrees with what the worker wants. It also assumes that the employee knows what is expected of him and that the organization will reward on the basis of productive effort instead of longevity, age, friendship or other factors that are often used.

While there have been a number of other theories, most are considered no more valid than the expectancy theory.

In view of the many and varied theories of motivation, it is no wonder that management guru Peter Drucker is quoted: "We know nothing about motivation. All we can do is write books about it."

There are, however, similarities in several of the theories discussed. They include factors that are related to the four conditions that must be present for a person to have high self-esteem.

CONNECTIVENESS:
> MASLOW: affection, belongingness, acceptance, friendship
> ALDERFER: meaningful social and, interpersonal relationships
> McGREGOR: (Y theory) good group relations
> McCLELLAN: need for affiliation; friendly, close interpersonal relationships
> HERZBERG: relationship with superiors and with peers

POWER:
> MASLOW: autonomy, self respect, self fulfillment, status
> McGREGOR: (Y theory) self-direction, self control
> McCLELLAN: need to excel, need for power
> HERZBERG: achievement, responsibility

UNIQUENESS:
>MASLOW: attention, recognition, self-esteem, self actualization
>McGREGOR: (Y theory) seeking responsibility, creativity
>HERZBERG: recognition, advancement, salary

MODELS:
>McCLELLAN: need to achieve relative to a set of standards.

It is obvious that there are elements of the four conditions that make up self-esteem within the theories outlined above. While none of the theories directly speak to the four conditions needed for self-esteem, there is enough evidence within them to provide a base for:

RICHARDSON'S SECOND LAW OF MOTIVATION:
Self-esteem is the greatest motivator.

Consider those with whom you have worked, as a peer, as a subordinate, or as a supervisor. Especially consider those who required little close supervision, those who were always ready to assume additional work and responsibility. They were probably the ones who advanced faster than most employees. If you were asked what single trait best described them, you would probably answer that they all had high self-esteem.

High self-esteem is the factor that gives some people the confidence to take on difficult tasks and enjoy working at a level that challenges their knowledge, skills, and talents. They can accept (temporarily) tasks that would seem menial and insulting to those with lower self-esteem. They require little effort on the part of the manager or supervisor in order to become motivated provided that certain factors are present in the work place.

WHAT DO WORKERS WANT IN THE WORK PLACE??

1. MEANINGFUL WORK. An employee will not be enthusiastic or motivated to carry out "make do" work. Self-esteem suffers when a person feels that he is not considered capable of doing work important to the aims of the organization.

2. ADEQUATE PAY FOR PERFORMANCE. While money is not high on the list of factors that affect motivation, it can become a <u>de</u>motivator if pay is not linked to performance. If an employee knows that a less effective worker is being paid more for a lower level of performance, she will be inclined to feel less enthusiastic toward the organization and the work.

3. ADEQUATE TRAINING. It is easy to bring in a new employee, show him his work station, and turn him loose to do the job. While it is easier and quicker, it does not serve the organization well unless the employee is highly experienced in the precise type work to be done. But even then, there may be differences in expectations of your organization and where the employee previously worked. There may be different parameters, different procedures or paperwork, or different standards of performance. Employees expect to be trained for their work so that they can be confident and competent to do the work. When the work changes significantly, the employee expects to be trained in order to be able to perform the new work. Remember: talking to someone is not training.

4. TWO-WAY COMMUNICATION. An employee expects to be TALKED WITH not just TALKED TO. Feedback should flow easily in both directions. Talking is only one part of the communication process. Listening is of greater importance in motivation.

5. RECOGNITION OF PERFORMANCE. Workers do not expect rewards beyond their regular pay for doing their work, but they do expect at least verbal recognition that they

are doing the work expected by management, not talked to only (and vociferously) when they make an error. If they are doing the job the way you hired them to do it, tell them so.

6. HELP IN SOLVING WORK PROBLEMS. This is not to imply that employees should never be told to "...see if you can work it out." It does mean that if the worker does not have the experience, training, or organization status to solve a particular problem, he should be able to get help from his supervisor or from management.

7. THE SAME ENTHUSIASM FOR THE WORK AND DEDICATION TO THE ORGANIZATION THAT MANAGEMENT EXPECTS FROM HER. (No further explanation is needed).

8. TRUST. Employees expect to be trusted, and they expect to be able to trust management. A major part of trust is the understanding on the part of the workers that their supervisor will follow through on commitments made to them.

9. LIMITS OF STRESS ON THE JOB. Nearly any job will be stressful from time to time, but constant stress (everything is rush or past due) will soon show its effect on performance. Nerves begin to fray and accuracy begins to decline. Managers who are stress addicted, and seem to get some kind of enjoyment from having employees work under stressful situations are those who also have a high rate of employee turnover. The unknown is one of the most insidious causes of stress for workers. If workers are told that ten percent of them will be fired (laid off, let go, terminated, suffer the consequences of "down-sizing", etc.) sometime in the near future, the effect on morale can be devastating. When morale sinks, motivation follows its plunge.

10. REALISTIC WORKLOAD. A frequent contributor to motivation and stress problems is unrealistic workload. One of America's most successful large corporations is known for setting performance standards that, while tough, are attainable. Management should never set goals that cannot be met, and should never assign workload that is unattainable. And only in emergency situations should they assign workloads that are

attainable only under stressful circumstances.

11. REASONABLE BUSINESS POLICIES. Workers understand that certain administrative policies are essential for the efficient and consistent operation of a business. But they do expect reasonable flexibility in these policies so that there is room for the occasional personal problem or recognition of the need for changing or updating those policies.

12. SUPERVISION WITHOUT OVER SUPERVISION. No one likes to have his supervisor constantly hovering over him checking to see if the Is are dotted and the Ts are crossed as he does his job. If the employee has been carefully selected for the job, has been trained and is fully capable of doing the work, he should be left alone to do it. Too close supervision delivers the message that the employee is not trusted or is not considered capable of doing the work on his own. (See 8. above)

13. SENSE OF CONNECTIVENESS. (Sounds familiar doesn't it?) Employees want to feel that they are an important part of the organization, not just one of many expendable, interchangeable, faceless, nameless entities represented by the smallest boxes at the lower levels of the organization chart and collectively referred to by those at the higher strata as "labor".

14. SENSE OF POWER. Employees want to know that, to some extent, they control their own destiny on the job, and that pay, advancement, retention, is based on performance. Favoritism; nepotism; retention and pay based solely on sex, race, longevity; are not practices that are conducive to neither a high level of motivation nor low rates of employee turnover.

15. SENSE OF UNIQUENESS. Employees want to be able to use their talents and skills in their work. By using each person's abilities to the fullest extent possible, the employee, the supervisor, and the organization all benefit.

16. SENSE OF ROLE MODELS. Both the supervisor and management should model the behavior, the enthusiasm, and the loyalty expected from the workers. Employees will

reflect the behavior of their bosses. In addition, workers expect models in the form of rules, regulations, and policies that provide strong, but not inflexible, guidelines.

17. WORKERS WANT TO KNOW WHAT THEY ARE TO DO, HOW TO DO IT, AND WHY THEY ARE TO DO IT. All of these bits of knowledge should be parts of the training process. The first two—what they are to do, and how they are to do it—are normally included in the entry training program. Unfortunately, the third is often neglected. Frequently, new employees are not told how the work they are going to do fits into the overall goals of the business. Let's visit again our old friends Sam and Sally (but let's also assume that they have been victims of consolidation, downsizing, streamlining, phase downs, or whatever term you prefer).

"Well, Sally, what do you do in your new job? Sam asked.

"I stick these little things called diodes—or transistors—or something through holes in this funny looking plastic thing and solder them in place," Sally replied.

"What are they for—what do they do?"

"I don't know, they use them in some kind of car, I think."

Wouldn't Sally feel better about herself, her job, and the company if she could have replied something like this?

"I build circuit boards that are used in the on-board computers that govern the fuel flow for the two-hundred horsepower engines used in the new Scatmobile XXI that will be introduced by Zipcar International on the seventeenth of September. I was shown one of the completed computers as part of my training. I saw videos of action shots of the Scatmobile XXI, and films showing how the computer controls the fuel flow, and how the fuel gets to the engine. I like working for Zipcar, it's a good company."

The training Sally was given and the open information policy of Zipmobile has made Sally feel important in her new role, and has made her an important unofficial spokesperson for the company. She has been told WHAT TO DO, HOW TO

DO IT, AND WHY THE WORK IS IMPORTANT TO THE ORGANIZATION. She wasn't told, "You do it because I told you to do it," or, "You do it because that's what we hired you to do."

18. IF THEY ARE NOT PERFORMING AS EXPECTED, THEY WANT TO BE TOLD WHAT THEY ARE NOT DOING AS EXPECTED AND HOW TO IMPROVE THEIR PERFORMANCE. I am aware of a department of a city where evaluations for promotions were made with a single composite score. The employees were only shown the final score although a number of factors and performance measurements were considered in arriving at the numerical rating. Workers were not told what factors were considered, in what areas they were deficient, nor what they could do to improve their rating. The results of this approach were frustration and suspicion that ratings were being manipulated in order that management could promote based on favoritism rather than aptitude.

Most of the problems with employee motivation are not caused by inadequacies in the individuals but by managers who expect workers to do things for which they are not prepared in terms of experience, education, or training. The primary motivational goal of a leader should be to provide his followers with whatever they need in order to become fully productive.

The eighteen items covered above are certainly not all inclusive, but they are factors that help employee self-esteem and, as a result, provide solid groundwork for them to be motivated to do the work. These are the things that workers need or want that would result in their being motivated and productive.

REMEMBER: Self-esteem and motivation are inseparable. As you help improve a person's self-esteem, you increase the likelihood that he will be motivated to do more and do better. This brings us to:

RICHARDSON'S THIRD LAW OF MOTIVATION.
Individuals are motivated—not groups.

To be successful in her efforts to build a work atmosphere in which workers are motivated, a supervisor/manager must realize that she has to deal with her subordinates individually. Under the ideal situation the leader serves as a mentor, cheerleader, and coach for each employee each day. This allows a close personal relationship with each employee. (This is a personal WORKING relationship, not a personal SOCIAL relationship. While, in some cases, there may be a social relationship, we are not speaking in those terms here).

The number of subordinates a person can normally supervise in these terms is about fifteen or sixteen. Any more makes daily personal contact and communication difficult.

Large group motivation involves the projection of a charismatic image with which most of the members of the group would like to identify. Note that we say MOST of the members of the group. As our efforts with the small group are aimed toward creating an atmosphere in which individuals tend to be motivated, so are our efforts in dealing with the large groups aimed toward the individual. The "RAH RAH" type speeches most of us have witnessed at one time or another at such places as large corporate gatherings or direct sales conventions do not affect each attendee equally. A few will react exuberantly and their production will increase immediately and continue at that level. Some will be enthusiastic for a period and their production will increase for that time, then level off a little higher than before. Some will be slightly affected without any increase in productivity. Others will sit with their arms crossed and tell themselves that the atmosphere is childish, may even be embarrassed, and will return to work with no better feelings toward their work or the organization.

````
`````

This is not to imply that you should not hold group meetings with your employees. Group meetings are an important part of the communication process. They are used to convey information that is of interest to all your employees, such as changes in rules and policies, to recognize performance, and to provide a sounding board for workers' thoughts, ideas, and gripes. Group meetings also provide cohesion for the group and a sense of connectiveness.

Your aim as a supervisor should be to work with your employees as closely as possible on a personal basis, and to provide to the extent possible considering your place in the organization those things wanted and needed by your workers for them to become fully productive.

FEAR AS A MOTIVATING TOOL

Fear can be a motivation tool, but only for short times in extreme circumstances...and NOT with employees. If somebody holds a gun to your head and tells you to give them all your money, your watch, your clothes, and the keys to your car, you will probably find yourself willingly standing naked in the street watching the bum dressed in your clothes and checking your watch drive away in your car. It could be less than wise—even disastrous—to attempt to dissuade him under those circumstances. The thug had you under his control ...and that is what fear is about. Fear is a control mechanism, not a method of motivating. Fear creates stress, which results in anxiety.

I have observed supervisors who felt that they had to keep their employees a little "off balance" or "on edge" by creating an atmosphere of fear in the organization. Their attitudes, their temper tantrums, and their (not always) subtle threats kept the workers wary of taking on new work, uncertain of their future with the organization, defensive. It destroyed their self-esteem. Other by products of the supervisors' attitudes was little or no dedication to the work, to the supervisor, or to the organization, high turnover; a lot of derogatory talk behind the bosses' backs; and an obvious display of relief whenever the boss was absent ...an event looked forward to by all members of the organization.

Those were the type of supervisors who referred to their employees as "dummies."

Nobody seems to have enough time. We all have the same twenty-four hours a day, but those who have learned to use their time wisely can accomplish more in their twenty-four. This is a valid booster of self-esteem. In the next chapter we will look at how effectively you use your time, and learn ways to make better use of it.

Chapter 15

THE PRESENT...IS GONE

What is the present now... is gone now. What was the present only seconds ago, is now the past. It can never be retrieved. Thus, it is important that we use it wisely.

"...never put off until tomorrow what you can do today," said Philip Dormer Stanhope, Fourth Earl of Chesterfield. This is a familiar quotation, but few people know it in its entirety.

"Know the true value of time: snatch, seize, and enjoy every moment of it. No idleness; no laziness; no procrastination; never put off until tomorrow what you can do today."

Apparently time was as valued and as wasted in the 1700's as it is today. We still do not have time to do all the things we want or need to do. We envy people who seem to have time to do everything; who seem to have more time than we have. Of course they have the same sixty seconds in a minute, the same sixty minutes in an hour, the same twenty-four hours in a day. Their secret is that they have learned to manage their time, to make better use of it. The object of this chapter is to help you learn to use your time more effectively, to plan the use of your time to get the most done, and to identify and get rid of time wasters. While this chapter will relate primarily to the work situation, the guidelines can be applied to your personal life as well.

What does time management have to do with self-esteem? When you learn how to manage your time most effectively you will be able to accomplish more of the things you want or need to do. When you accomplish more you feel better about yourself.

THREE CHARACTERISTICS OF TIME:
1. Time can be measured; therefore, it can be apportioned.
2. Time is always passing, but once past, it can never be regained.
3. Time can be used well or wasted.

Because time can be measured, we can plan and schedule our activities. Experience can be used to estimate time required to perform tasks. However, when using experience as a gauge for future efforts, be sure to question how well you used your time in doing the work. Did you use your time wisely when doing those tasks, or did you fall prey to Northcote Parkinson's "law" which states: "Work expands so as to fill the time available for its completion."

As covered in the beginning of this chapter, time can never be retrieved. The late stand-up comedian and home-spun philosopher Dave Gardner said, "...you can't do something again—you can do something similar."

People, as they grow older, tend to become more aware of the time they wasted in the past and the ever-lessening time available in their future. Unfortunately, this doesn't necessarily mean that they will use that future any more wisely than they used their time in the past. It behooves us to use time effectively, no matter what our age.

"I would I could stand on a busy corner, hat in hand, and beg people to throw me all their wasted hours."
        Bernard Berenson
        (Strange wording, but it gets the point across)

HOW ARE YOU SPENDING YOUR TIME?

To learn to manage your time, take a good look at how you spend your time. Look at your work; look at yourself.

Start by keeping an informal log of how you spend

your time at work. Forms have been designed for this, but some are so detailed that maintaining them can take too much time. Instead, make your own. Draw lines down a sheet of lined paper to make enough columns for the primary tasks you perform each day. Make extra columns for those things that seem to crop up that are outside your normal duties. Make up enough of these sheets to last two weeks.

Whenever you complete a task make a quick note under the proper heading, giving just enough detail to give whatever identification you feel necessary for a review after two weeks. With each entry write down the hours/ minutes spent on that activity. Start a new sheet each day for a minimum of two weeks, longer if you feel that you should to have a good record of all your normal activities. Date each sheet.

Be honest. Write down the water cooler chats, personal telephone calls, and the time spent on them, just as honestly as the most important work you do.

When you are satisfied that you have maintained your log for a long enough period, you are ready to begin the analysis of your activities. What do you ask yourself about your activities?

1. WHAT AM I DOING THAT DOES NOT HAVE TO BE DONE?

Sometimes we find ourselves doing things simply because nobody ever told us to stop. Other times we find that we have taken on some tasks because they were necessary at one time, and never stopped. Are you doing unnecessary reviews, checks, and repetitive calculations? If you find things that are unnecessary, stop doing them if it is within your authority to do so. If not, ask your supervisor. You may need to demonstrate a degree of assertiveness. If your supervisor/manager hums and haws, tell her how much time the tasks are taking, and press for a definite answer.

2. HOW MUCH NON-PRODUCTIVE TIME DOES MY LOG SHOW?

It doesn't take much analysis to find out if you are spending too much time on activities that do not contribute to the work of the organization. It is unlikely that you will ever be able to eliminate all non-productive activities, but you will be able to reduce them. You may feel a trifle guilty when you see how much of your time is non-productive.

3. AM I DOING THINGS THAT SHOULD BE DONE BY SOMEONE ELSE?

A good analysis might show that some of the things you do would better align with the work done by someone else. You may find that you have to get information from another person in order to do a task. It might be that the other person could do the work in less time because he has the needed information readily available. Perhaps you are doing some things that could be done by a lower paid employee.

Often, when organizations are starting out, employees are used as Jacks/Jills-of-all-trades, doing a lot of varied tasks. As the business grows, additional people—many of them specialists with particular skills—are hired, but the existing jobs are not reviewed and tasks realigned between the old and the new employees. This is a good time to impress your boss by pointing out work that should be shifted about.

4. WHAT AM I DOING THAT COULD BE DONE MORE EFFICIENTLY?

We tend to get into ruts and never take time to look at the way we do our work; we just do it the way we have always done it. Look for shortcuts. Look for ways of using some of those laborsaving devices that show up sooner or later in any business.

Vilfredo Pareto, nineteenth century Italian economist, stated that the significant items in a given group normally constitute a relatively small portion of the total items in a group. In plain English, about twenty percent of the things you do take about eighty percent of your time. This means that by using the log you kept for two weeks or so, you should be able to identify the twenty percent of your activities that take up eighty percent of your time. Those are the activities that you should target for more efficient and effective methods.

NOTE: The Pareto principle applies to most areas of your life and your work. A simple study would show that about eighty percent of your money is spent on about twenty percent of your expenses; that some eighty percent of the problems in your organization are caused by some twenty percent of your workers; eighty percent of the errors are made by twenty percent of your employees.

Now that you have identified the twenty percent of your activities that account for eighty percent of your time, let's take a look at some of the ways you can save time on that twenty percent. This list cannot be all-inclusive because there are so many ways we earn our livings.

MOTION ECONOMY:

During the early years of this century Frank Gilbreth gave up a career as a construction contractor to study scientific management, a rigid, tightly controlled management style developed by Fredrick Winslow Taylor. Taylor's work resulted in the time study. His efforts were more fully developed by Dr. Ralph M. Barnes. While the principles of motion economy were originally aimed at reducing fatigue and increasing efficiency of workers involved in manual labor—particularly in the manufacturing and construction fields—they can also be applied to any type work: reduce the finger, hand, arm, body movements and, where possible, utilize simultaneous, similar motions made by both hands. Consider the layout of work areas—including your own—and ask a few simple questions:

> *Are workstations designed so that a minimum of motion is required to reach tools, material, and
> *Are tools and materials easily accessible to workers?

*Is the work area designed to eliminate bottlenecks?
*Are workers who deal with visitors nearest the entrance?
*Is work distributed evenly?
*Does the work area layout facilitate supervision?
*Does work flow through the work area without back tracking?
*Are workers with frequent contact located near each other?
*Is YOUR work area (desk) arranged for economy of motion?
*Is your desk arranged so that the tools and materials used most often are readily available?
*Are most-used records and files readily accessible?
*Do you have to HUNT for things too often in your own work area or desk?
*Are drawers, in baskets, files, jumbled and filled with things you may never need?

While this is a short list, it should give an insight into the kinds of things you should search out to provide the most efficient, timesaving work place.

MEETINGS:
*Avoid unnecessary meetings.
*Don't call for meetings when individual, face-to-face communication would better serve your need.
*Set time schedules for meetings.
*Invite only those who need to attend.
*Consider stand-up meetings. People don't talk as long when they are standing as when seated.
*Stick to the agenda.
*Don't make the meeting place too comfortable.

TELEPHONE:
*Let your secretary screen out unnecessary calls.

*Tell long-winded callers you will call them back so you can control time spent on the call.
*Stand up when talking or making a call.
*Keep on the subject.
*Group outgoing calls.
*Make notes before calling to help you cover everything and stay on subject.
*Tell callers who want to chat that you have important work to do and excuse yourself. (Some who are people-oriented fear hurting others' feelings by cutting off telephone conversations ...remember, it is your job and your time you will be saving.)

VISITORS:
*Tell visitor that you can only be available for a certain amount of time (assuming she is not your boss).
*Stay standing—he will likely do the same. When business is completed, start moving toward the door.
*When doing important work, close your office door and let your secretary screen potential visitors.
*Keep visitor—and yourself—on the subject.
*Go to the other person's office if she is a timewaster. You can control the visit.
*Tell the visitor you have important work and excuse yourself.
*In the case of the important, long-winded visitor, arrange with your secretary for her to call you on the phone after a specified period of time. (This may sound underhanded, but it can be effective if the visitor doesn't know it is your secretary who is calling.)

OTHER TIME SAVERS:
*Delegate.
*Learn problem-solving/decision-making techniques.
*Improve communication skills.
*Don't be a perfectionist. Must a simple memo to

someone within the organization be redone because of a typo that could be corrected with a pen?

ONE OF THE MOST IMPORTANT TIME SAVERS: LEARN TO SAY NO!!!

The person who hasn't learned to say NO is most likely the person who complains most about not having enough time. Again, the people-oriented person may fear hurting someone's feelings, but you must consider your own interests and needs. If you feel too pushed and there are others who could take on the task, say no. If there are NOT others who know how to carry out the task, still say NO if you don't think you can take on the work. Let someone else take on the task and feel good about doing something new.

As a part of learning to say N0, also learn not to let the monkey jump on your back. THE MONKEY?? There is an old story about a lady walking down the hall when a co-worker approaches from the other direction. The co-worker has a monkey on his shoulder. The co-worker stops and says, "I have this monkey on my shoulder and I don't know how to get rid of it. It really bothers me."

The lady says, "I'll take care of it." and the monkey jumps on her shoulder. The co-worker walks away unburdened, and the lady walks away with the monkey on her shoulder ...something else to worry about and consume her time. The moral is, of course, don't volunteer to take on other people's problems.

What could the lady have done? She could have asked, "Have you tried such-and-such? How about trying this...? Let me suggest that you..." She could have given helpful guidance without assuming responsibility. If she honestly could not offer advice this would be another alternative. "You sure have a problem there. I don't know how I could help. Let me know how you get rid of it."

THE FIFTEEN-MINUTE TASK

Most people would never risk telling their boss NO when she wants to assign additional work that, "...will only take about fifteen minutes a week." Those "fifteen-minute" jobs have a way of growing like a cup of rice dumped into a pot of boiling water. Let's assume that your boss approaches you and says she has this little weekly report that has to be done every week. You can only do about a third of the work you put down on your daily work schedule, you have been donating several hours of overtime a week and taking work home on the weekend.

"Fifteen minutes a week is all it will take," she says.

You think: Well, ok I guess I can squeeze it into my week ...besides, the boss wants me to do it and she IS the boss.

Friday comes and the report is due so you show fifteen minutes on your work schedule. You just have to go down the hall to Jack's office and get the needed data.

Jack listens to you describe what you need and then shakes his head. "I don't work with the data in that format," he says, "I can dig up the figures, but you will have to work out the statistics. And I only work with part of what you need. You'll have to get this part from Sally and that information from Sam."

Sally is helpful at first, then gives an answer you don't need to hear, "I don't get these production figures until last thing each Friday. No way can I get them sooner. Most of them come from offices across the country. Because of the different time zones..."

Sam isn't even that helpful. "Another damned report? I don't have time to look up all that garbage. If you have to have it, you can go through this printout I get each Monday and look it up for yourself." He pushes a six-inch stack of manifold printout across his desk. It is the fifth carbon copy, and the 3's, 5's, 6's, 8's, and 9's are all alike...rounded smudges.

You realize that the "...little fifteen minute report" is a major undertaking that will take hours instead of minutes.

ˎˎˎˎ

You are sitting at your desk, your head feeling like a concrete mixer when your boss walks up, smiles, and asks, "Is that little report all ready for me?"

Which is your response?
1. "I'm working on it, but this being the first time, it's taking a little longer than I expected.
2. "No, it is not ready. You're going to have to find somebody else to take on this work. Let me explain why I do not have the time to do it." Tell her your experience in trying to get the needed information, suggest that the content of the report be reconsidered.
3. Jump out the nearest window.

I recommend response number 2. Understand that you must let your boss know the consequences of taking on the work: other work will have to be sacrificed or assigned to someone else. This is a form of self-protection that you owe yourself. You said N0, and you told her why.

ENERGY CYCLES:

Our energy runs in cycles during the day. At some times our energy is high and at other times it is low. These cycles are fairly consistent from day to day. You can become aware of your energy levels by keeping another log divided into four or five time segments during the day and evening. Rate yourself on a scale of 1 to 10 for each time segment, a 1 representing a period of low energy, and a 10 representing the highest. Keep this up for a couple of weeks. Then, chart your highs and lows for a typical day.

Using your chart as a pattern, schedule your most demanding tasks for those times of the day when your energy is high and the less demanding tasks for low periods.

PROCRASTINATION:

People procrastinate for three reasons:
*They find the task unpleasant
*They don't consider themselves competent to do the

task

*They lack confidence in themselves.

Procrastination is a time-waster because we often fill the time we would take to do the task with less important work or simply goof off to avoid facing the task.

A cure for procrastination is to break the task into steps that are individually less demanding. Make each step a goal. Each of these goals is less formidable than the overall task. Congratulate yourself as you complete each step. If the task is assigned by your boss and you truly do not feel competent to do the work, don't hesitate to tell your boss and ask for additional training. It is better to tell your boss that you don't think you can handle the work than to grope your way along and possibly turn out an unacceptable piece of work.

GET ORGANIZED:

Organization is a great time saver. Three parts of work organization are:
1. Planning
2. Prioritizing
3. Scheduling

First thing each morning write down the tasks you want to do that day. Give each a priority rating starting with number one for the most important and continuing through your list to the least important. Next, based on your best information, estimate the time each task will take. With your energy peaks and valleys in mind schedule the work through the day. Be aware that the most important may not be the first thing to be done unless it is very important that it be done early. The early hours may be a time of low energy. Plan to finish some less demanding tasks so that you can tackle the more important ones when your energy is high.

DON'T OVERBOOK YOUR DAILY WORK SCHEDULE.

Be aware that there must be flexibility in your schedule. Don't be upset if you can't accomplish every thing on your schedule. Because of unforeseen interruptions, you can make a "hard" schedule for only about fifty percent your time. Just remember that the task you assigned number one priority remains number one. If you must trim your schedule, begin by scratching from your list those tasks you gave the lowest priority. They may be the tasks that you have to "...put off until tomorrow..."

Chapter 16

WHAT HAVE YOU DONE?
WHAT ARE YOU GOING TO DO?

Through the preceding chapters we have discussed what self-esteem is, how our level of self-esteem is developed, what to do about things we do not like about ourselves, and how we can work with employees in ways that build their self-esteem.

Now it's time to look at how you have applied what you have learned. Have you done things that improve your own self-esteem? Have you worked with your employees in ways that build their self-esteem—or at the least have not caused damage to their self-esteem? Are you more aware of the importance of their maintaining a healthy self-esteem in order for them to be motivated and fully productive?

This is the time to perform a bit of introspection. Take a little time to answer the following:

WHAT HAVE I DONE TO ENHANCE MY OWN SELF-ESTEEM SINCE I BEGAN READING THIS BOOK?

WHAT HAVE I DONE TO ENHANCE MY WORKERS' SELF-ESTEEM SINCE I BEGAN READING THIS BOOK?

WHAT ARE YOUR GOALS FOR THE NEXT THREE MONTHS, SIX MONTHS, AND YEAR FOR ENHANCING YOUR OWN SELF-ESTEEM?

WHAT ARE YOUR GOALS FOR ENHANCING YOUR WORKERS' SELF-ESTEEM?

WHAT ELSE?

The principals and practices outlined in this book are applicable to other parts of your life as well as at work. Consider your wife, husband, girl friend, boy friend, siblings, children and, yes, even perfect strangers. Remember that the way you act or react to them can positively or negatively affect their self–esteem. Don't treat your workers better than you treat the folks at home.

I sincerely hope that you have found this book valuable and that you have applied what you have learned. If you have comments, questions, or suggestions concerning material in the book, feel free to email me at: *jrichard35@cfl.rr.com*

Works Consulted:

Branden, Nathanial, PhD. The Psychology of High Self-Esteem. Nightingale-Conant Corp. Chicago, IL

Byham, William C. Ph.D. Jeff Cox. Zapp! The Lightning of Empowerment. New York: Fawcett Columbine Books. 1988.

Clemes, Harris, Ph.D., Reynold Bean. How To Raise Your Children's Self-Esteem. San Jose, California: OHAUS. 1978.

Clemes, Harris, Ph.D., Reynold Bean. How To Raise Teenagers' Self-Esteem. Los Angeles, California: Price Stern Sloan. 1990.

Clemes, Harris, Ph.D., Reynold Bean. How To Teach Children Responsibility. Los AngeleCalifornia: Price Stern Sloan. 1990

Crosby, Philip B. Quality Without Tears: The Art of Hassle-Free Management. New York: Plume Books. 1984.

Fulmer, Robert M. The New Management. New York. Mcmillan Publishing Co., Inc. 1974.

Harrell, Thomas Willard. Industrial Psychology. New York: Holt, Rinehart and Wilson. 1960.

Hodges, Henry G., Ph.D. Management: Principles, Practices, Problems. Cambridge, Massachusetts, 1956.

Lakein, Alan. How to Get Control of Your Time and Your Life. New York: Signet Books. 1973.

Lazarus, Arnold, Ph.D., Allen Fay, M.D. I Can if I Want To. New York: Warner Books. 1975.

Mackenzie, R. Alec. <u>The Time trap: How to Get More Done in Less Time</u>. New York: McGraw-Hill. 1972.

McKay, Matthew, Ph.D. Patrick Fanning. <u>Self-Esteem</u>. Oakland, California. New Harbinger Publications. 1987.

Newman, William H. <u>Administrative Action:The Techniques of Organization and Management:</u> Englewood Cliffs, New Jersey, 1950

Pascale, Richard T., Anthony G. Athos. <u>The Art of Japanese Management Applications for American Executives</u> New York: Warner Books. 1981.

Peale, Norman Vincent. <u>THE Power of Positive Thinking</u> Englewood Cliffs, New Jersey: Prentice Hall, Inc. 1978.

Peck, M. Scott, M.D. <u>The Road Less Traveled: A new Psychology of Love, Traditional Values and Spiritual Growth.</u> New York: Simon and Schuster. 1978.

Peters, Thomas J., Robert H. Waterman. <u>In Search of Excellence: Lessons from America's Best-Run Companies.</u> New York: Harper and Row. 1982.

Peters, Tom. <u>Thriving on Chaos: Handbook for a Management Revolution</u>. New York: Alfred A. Knopf. 1987.

Plunkett, Lorne C., Guy A. Hale. <u>The Proactive Manager: The Complete Book of Problem Solving and Decision Making.</u> New York: John Wiley and Sons. 1982.

Robbins, Stephen P. <u>The Administrative Process</u>. Englewood Cliffs, New Jersey: Prentice-Hall, 1980.

Sarnoff, Dorothy, Gaylen Moore. <u>Never Be Nervous Again: TimeTested Techniques for the Foolproof Control of Nervousness in Communicating Situations.</u> New York: Ballantine Books. 1987.

Schuller, Robert H<u>.</u> <u>Self Love</u>. Old Tappen, New Jersey: 1969.

Steers, Richard M., Lyman W. Porter. <u>Motivation and Work Behavior.</u> New York: McGraw-Hill Book Company. 1983.

Szilagyi, Andrew D. Jr. Marc J. Wallace, Jr., <u>Organizational Behavior and Performance</u>. Glenview Illinois: Scott, Foresman and Company. 1980.

Waitley, Denis, Ph.D<u>. Seeds of Greatness</u>. New York: Simon & Schuster. 1983.

Waitley, Denis, Ph.D. <u>The Psychology of Winning: Ten Qualities of a Total Winner</u>. New York: The Berkley Publishing Group. 1984.

Ziglar, Zig. <u>Top Performance: How to Develop Excellence in Yourself and Others</u>. New York: Berkley Books. 1987.

Zimbardo, Philip G. <u>Shyness: What It Is, What To Do About It.</u> New York: Jove Publications, Inc. 1977.

To order quantities of this book please contact the author for price including shipping:

Jrichard35@cfl.rr.com
Or
Telephone
321-269-3972

Made in the USA
Lexington, KY
20 September 2018